Three Chord Songs

ISBN 978-1-4584-1103-7

HAL•LEONARD®
CORPORATION

7777 W. BLUEMOUND RD. P.O. BOX 13819 MILWAUKEE, WI 53213

Visit Hal Leonard Online at
www.halleonard.com

Ukulele Chord Songbook

Contents

All Along the Watchtower

Words and Music by
Bob Dylan

There must be some kind a way out-ta here, ___

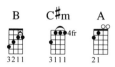

B   C#m   A

3211   3111   21

Intro

B C#m	B A	B C#m	B A
	B	C#m B	A B	
C#m B	A B		

Verse 1

C#m   B   A   B
There must be some kind a way outta here,

C#m   B   A   B
Say the jok-er to the thief.

C#m   B   A   B
There's too much confusion,

C#m B   A   B
I can't get no re-lief.

C#m   B   A   B
Business men, they, ah, drink my wine.

C#m   B   A   B
Plow man, dig my earth.

C#m   B   A   B
None will level on ___ the line,

C#m   B   A
Nobody of it is worth. ___ Hey, hey!

Guitar Solo 1   ‖: C#m   B | A   B   :‖ *Play 4 times*

Verse 2

C#m   B   A   B
No reason to get excit-ed,

C#m   B   A   B
The thief, he kindly spoke.

C#m   B   A   B
There are man-y here among us

C#m   B   A   B
Who feel that life ____ is but a joke.

C#m   B   A
But, uh,   but you and I, we've been ____ through that,

B   C#m   B   A   B
But, ah,   and this is not our fate.

C#m   B   A   B
So let us not talk false - ly now,

C#m   B   A   B
The hour's gettin' late, ____ ah. Hey!

Guitar Solo 2   ‖: C#m   B | A   B   :‖ *Play 4 times*

Interlude   ‖: C#m   B | A   B   :‖ *Play 3 times*
    | C#m   B | A   B |
                    Hey!

Guitar Solo 3   ‖: C#m   B |A   B   :‖ *Play 8 times*

                    C#m B   A   B
Verse 3   Well, all a-long the watch - tower,
                    C#m   B   A   B
                      Princes kept the view.
                    C#m   B   A   B
                      While all the women came ___ and went,
                    C#m   B   A
                      Bare feet servants too.
                    B   C#m   B   A   B
                      Well, ah, oh, outside in the cold distance, uh,
                    C#m   B   A   B
                      A wild cat   did growl.
                    C#m   B   A   B
                      Two riders were approachin'
                              C#m   B   A   B
                    And the wind be-gan to howl.   Hey!

Outro   ‖: C#m   B |A   B   :‖ *Repeat and fade*
                                                   (w/voc. ad lib.)

All Right Now

Words and Music by
Andy Fraser and Paul Rodgers

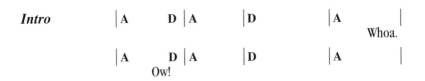

Intro

| A   D | A | D | A |

Whoa.

| A   D | A | D | A |

Ow!

Verse 1

       A   D A
There she stood in the street,

    D   A
Smil - in' from her head to her feet.

            D A
I said a, "Hey, now, what is this?

           D   A
Now, baby, maybe, may - be she's in need of a kiss."

         D   A
I said a, "Hey, uh-huh, what's your name, baby?

   D   A
May - be we can see things the same.

          D   A
Now don't you wait or ____ hesitate.

    D   A
Let's move ____ before they raise the parking rate." Ow!

Chorus 1

   A   G   D   A
All right ___ now. Baby, it's all ___ right now.

            G   D   A
All right ___ now. Baby, it's all ___ right now, ___ woh.

   A   D   A   D   A
   Let me tell ya now.   Oo, ah.

Verse 2

                             A   D A
I took her home ___ to my place,

           D   A
Watch - in' ev'ry move on her face.

                     D   A
She said, "Look, what's your game, baby?

         D   A
Are ___ you try'n' to put me in shame?"

                   D   A
I said a, "Slow, don't go so fast.

          D   A
Don't ___ you think that love can last?"

                     D   A
She said, "Love? Lord ___ a-bove.

           D   A
Oo. Now ___ you're try'n' to trick me in love." Ow!

Chorus 2

   A   G   D   A
All right ___ now. Baby, it's all ___ right now.

            G   D   A
All right ___ now. Baby, it's all ___ right now.

Yeah, it's all right now.

Guitar Solo 1 | A | | | |
                      | | | | |

Interlude | A | G D | A | G D |

Bridge

    A   D   A   D
Ow!

    A
      Let me tell you all about it now.

      D   A   D   A
Ow!   Yeah.

Verse 3   *Repeat Verse 2*

Chorus 3

    A   G   D   A
All right ___ now. Baby, it's all ___ right now.
         G   D   A
All right ___ now. Baby, it's all ___ right now.

Outro

    A   G   D A
    All right now. Baby, it's all ___ right.

         G
Yeah, all right now.

  D   A
Baby, baby, baby, it's all right.

        G
All, all right now. Yeah.

  D   A
It's all right, it's all right, it's all right, yeah, huh.

        G   D   A
All right now. Baby, it's all ___ right now.

         G
Yeah, we're so happy together. Ow!

  D   A
It's all right, it's all right, it's all right.

           G   D   A
Ev'rything's all right. Yeah.   Woo!

All Shook Up

Words and Music by
Otis Blackwell and Elvis Presley

Melody:

A well a bless my soul, __ what's...

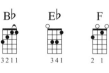

3 2 1 1   3 4 1   2 1

Intro | Bb | | | |

Verse 1
              Bb
A well a bless my soul, what's wrong with me?

I'm itching like a man on a fuzzy tree.

My friends say I'm actin' wild as a bug.
             N.C.
I'm in love.

I'm all shook up!

       Eb   **F**   **Bb**
Mm, mm, ooh, ooh, yeah,__ yeah, yeah!

Verse 2
              Bb
My hands are shaky and my knees are weak

I can't seem to stand on my own two feet.

Who do you thank when you have such luck?
             N.C.
I'm in love.

I'm all shook up!

       Eb   **F**   **Bb**
Mm, mm, ooh, ooh, yeah,__ yeah, yeah!

Bridge 1

      E♭
Well, please___ don't ask me what's a on my mind,

    B♭
I'm a little mixed up but I feel fine.

    E♭
When I'm near that girl that I love best,

   F **N.C.**
My heart beats so it scares me to death!

      B♭
Verse 3 She touched___ my hand, what a chill I got.

Her kisses are like a volcano that's hot!

I'm proud to say that she's my buttercup.

     N.C.
I'm in love.

I'm all shook up!

   E♭   **F**   **B♭**
Mm, mm, ooh, ooh, yeah,___ yeah, yeah!

Bridge 2

E♭
My tongue gets tied when I try to speak,

B♭
My insides shake like a leaf on a tree.

E♭
There's only one cure for this soul of mine,

F N.C.
That's to have the girl that I love so fine!

Verse 4

B♭
She touched__ my hand, what a chill I got.

Her kisses are like a volcano that's hot!

I'm proud to say that she's my buttercup.

N.C.
I'm in love.

I'm all shook up!

E♭   F   B♭
Mm, mm, ooh, ooh, yeah,__ yeah, yeah!

E♭   F   B♭
Mm, mm, ooh, ooh, yeah,__ yeah,

I'm all shook up!

Authority Song

Words and Music by
John Mellencamp

Melody:

They __ like to get you in a

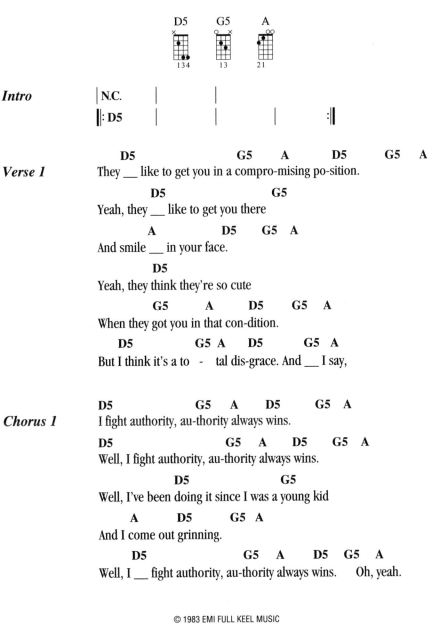

D5   G5   A

Intro | N.C. | |

‖: D5 | | | :‖

Verse 1

     D5   G5 A   D5   G5 A
They __ like to get you in a compro-mising po-sition.

     D5   G5
Yeah, they __ like to get you there

    A   D5 G5 A
And smile __ in your face.

      D5
Yeah, they think they're so cute

      G5   A   D5 G5 A
When they got you in that con-dition.

     D5   G5 A D5   G5 A
But I think it's a to -   tal dis-grace. And __ I say,

Chorus 1

D5   G5 A   D5   G5 A
I fight authority, au-thority always wins.

D5   G5 A   D5 G5 A
Well, I fight authority, au-thority always wins.

       D5   G5
Well, I've been doing it since I was a young kid

     A   D5   G5 A
And I come out grinning.

      D5   G5 A   D5 G5 A
Well, I __ fight authority, au-thority always wins.   Oh, yeah.

Interlude 1   ‖: D5 | G5 A   :‖

Verse 2
                    D5   G5
            I call up my preacher, I say,

                        A   D5   G5   A
            "Give me strength for round __ five."

                        D5   G5
            He said, "You don't need no strength,

                        A   D5   G5   A
            You need to grow up, son."

                        D5   G5   A   D5   G5   A
            I said, "Growing up leads to grow - ing old and then to dying.

                        D5   G5   A   D5
            Ooh, and dying to me don't sound ____ like all that much fun."

                        G5 A
            And so I say,

Chorus 2
                    D5   G5   A   D5   G5   A
            I fight authority, au-thority always wins.

                        D5   G5   A   D5   G5 A
            Well, I __ fight authority, au-thority always wins.

                        D5   G5
            Well, I've been doing it since I was a young kid;

            A   D5   G5 A
            I've come out grinning.

                        D5   G5   A   D5   G5   A
            Well, I __ fight authority, au-thority always wins.

Guitar Solo　　　‖: D5　　　| G5　A　:‖　*Play 8 times*

Interlude 2

　　　　　　　　　N.C.
I say oh, ＿＿ no, no, no.

I say oh, no, no, no.

I say oh, no, no, no, no.

Chorus 3

N.C.
I fight authority, authority always wins.

I fight authority, authority always wins. Kick it in.

　　　　　　D5　　　　　　　　　　　G5
I've been doing it since I was a young kid

　　　　　　　A　　　　D5　　　G5　A
And I've come out grinning.

Outro

　　　　　　D5
Well, I ＿ fight authority,

　　　　G5　　A　　　D5　　G5　A
Au-thority always wins.

‖:　　　D5
　　Well, I ＿ fight authority,

　　　　G5　　A　　　D5　　G5　A　:‖　*Repeat and fade*
Au-thority always wins.

Bad Case of Loving You

Words and Music by
John Moon Martin

Melody:

The hot sum-mer night ___

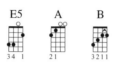

E5   A   B

3 4 1   2 1   3 2 1 1

Intro   ‖: E5 | :‖ *Play 4 times*

Verse 1
                              E5
The hot summer night fell like a net;

            A   B   E5
I gotta find ____ my baby yet.

I need   you to sooth my head,

            A   B   E5
To turn my blue ____ heart to red.

Chorus 1
          E5   N.C.
Doctor, doctor gimme the news

          E5 N.C.
I got a   bad case of loving you.

          A
    No pill's gonna cure my ill,

          E5   B
I got a   bad case of lovin' you.

Interlude 1   ‖: E5 | :‖

Verse 2

          E5
A pretty face, don't make no pretty heart.

       A   **B**   **E5**
I learned that,   buddy, from the start.

You think I'm cute, a little bit shy,

      A B   **E5**
Mama, I ain't that kind of guy.

Chorus 2   *Repeat Chorus 1*

Guitar Solo

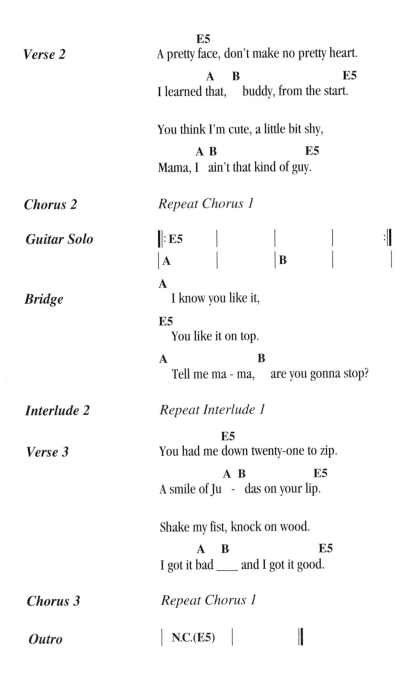

Bridge

A
   I know you like it,

E5
   You like it on top.

A   **B**
   Tell me ma - ma,   are you gonna stop?

Interlude 2   *Repeat Interlude 1*

Verse 3

            E5
You had me down twenty-one to zip.

        A B   **E5**
A smile of Ju - das on your lip.

Shake my fist, knock on wood.

       A   **B**   **E5**
I got it bad ____ and I got it good.

Chorus 3   *Repeat Chorus 1*

Outro | N.C.(E5) | ‖

The Ballad of John and Yoko

Words and Music by
John Lennon and Paul McCartney

Melody:

Stand-ing in the dock at South Hamp - ton,

E   A   B7

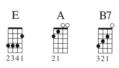

2341   21   321

Intro

| E | | |

Verse 1

E
Standing in the dock at South Hampton,

Trying to get to Holland or France.

The man in the mac said,

"You've got to go back,"

You know they didn't give us a chance.

Chorus 1

        A
Christ! You know it ain't easy,
         E
You know how hard it can be,
       B7
The way things are going,
      E
They're gonna crucify me.

Verse 2	**E** Finally made the plane into Paris,
	Honeymooning down by the Seine.
	Peter Brown called to say,
	"You can make it OK,
	You can get married in Gibraltar, near Spain."
Chorus 2	*Repeat Chorus 1*
Verse 3	**E** Drove from Paris to the Amsterdam Hilton,
	Talking in our beds for a week.
	The newspeople said,
	"Say, what you doing in bed?"
	I said, "We're only trying to get us some peace."
Chorus 3	*Repeat Chorus 1*
Bridge	**A** Saving up your money for a rainy day,
	Giving all your clothes to charity.
	Last night the wife said,
	"Oh boy, when you're dead,
	B7 You don't take nothing with you but your soul."
	Think!

Verse 4

E
Made a lightning trip to Vienna,

Eating chocolate cake in a bag.

The newspapers said,

"She's gone to his head,

They look just like two gurus in drag."

Chorus 4   *Repeat Chorus 1*

Verse 5

E
Caught the early plane back to London,

Fifty acorns tied in a sack.

The men from the press said,

"We wish you success,

It's good to have the both of you back."

Chorus 5

A
Christ! You know it ain't easy,

E
You know how hard it can be,

B7
The way things are going,

E
They're gonna crucify me.

B7
The way things are going,

E
They're gonna crucify me.

| B7 | | E | ‖

Bang a Gong
(Get It On)

Words and Music by
Marc Bolan

Melody:

Well, you're dirt - y and sweet,

E5   A5   G5

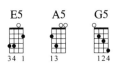

Intro   ‖: E5 | | | :‖

Verse 1

          E5   **A5**
Well, you're dirt - y and sweet, clad in black,

                     E5
Don't look back, and I love __ you.

      A5   **E5**
You're dirty and sweet, oh yeah.

Well, you're slim and you're weak,

           A5   **E5**
You've got the teeth of the hydra upon __ you.

      A5   **E5**
You're dirty, sweet and you're my girl.

Chorus 1

        G5   **A5**   **E5**
Get it on. ____ Bang a gong. ____ Get it on.

        G5   **A5**   **E5**
Get it on. ____ Bang a gong. ____ Get it on.

Verse 2

                      E5
Well, you're built __ like a car,

          A5   E5
You've got a hubcap diamond star ha - lo.

        A5   E5
You're built like a car, oh yeah.

                             A5
Well, you're an untamed youth, that's the truth,

                E5
With your cloak full of ea - gles.

      A5   E5
You're dirty, sweet and you're my girl.

Chorus 2   *Repeat Chorus 1*

Verse 3

                    E5
Well, you're wind - y and wild,

          A5   E5
You've got the blues in your shoes and your stock - ings.

        A5   E5
You're windy and wild, oh yeah.

Well, you're built like a car,

        A5   E5
You've got a hubcap diamond star ha - lo.

        A5   E5
You're dirty, sweet and you're my girl.

Chorus 3   *Repeat Chorus 1*

Interlude 1 | E5 | | | |

                     | | | | |

Verse 4

E5
Well, you're dirt - y and sweet, clad in black,
A5   E5
Don't look back and I love __ you.
  A5   E5
You're dirty and sweet, oh yeah.

Well, you dance when you walk,
        A5   E5
So let's dance, ____ take a chance, understand ____ me.
    A5   E5
You're dirty, sweet and you're my girl.

Chorus 4

       G5   A5   E5
Get it on. ____ Bang a gong. ____ Get it on.
       G5   A5   E5
Get it on. ____ Bang a gong. ____ Get it on.   Ow!
       G5   A5   E5
Get it on. ____ Bang a gong. ____ Get it on.   Ow!

Interlude 2 | E5 | | | |

Sax Solo | E5 | | | |

Chorus 5

       G5   A5
Get it on. ____ Bang a gong. ____ Get it on.
E5
  Uh, uh, uh, uh, uh, uh.
       G5   A5
Get it on. ____ Bang a gong. ____ Get it on.
E5
  Uh, uh, uh, uh, uh.
       G5   A5
Get it on. ____ Bang a gong. ____ Get it on.
E5
  Uh, uh, uh, uh, uh, uh.
       G5   A5   E5
Get it on. ____ Bang a gong. ____ Get it on.   *Take me.*

Outro | G5 | A5 | E5 | | |

‖: E5 | :‖ *Repeat and fade*

Barbara Ann

Words and Music by
Fred Fassert

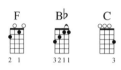

Chorus 1

N.C.
(Ba, ba, ba, ba, Ba'bra Ann.

Ba, ba, ba, ba, Ba'bra Ann.)

      F   Bb
Ba'bra Ann, take my hand.

      F   C
Ba'bra Ann, you got me rockin' and a rollin',

 Bb   F
Rock - in' and a reelin', Ba'bra Ann,

Ba, ba, ba, Ba'bra Ann.

Verse 1

F
Went to a dance, lookin' for romance,

Saw Ba'bra Ann, so I thought I'd take a chance.

      Bb
Oh, Ba'bra Ann, Ba'bra Ann, take my hand.

      F
Oh, Ba'bra Ann, Ba'bra Ann, take my hand.

      C
You got me rockin' and a rollin',

 Bb   F
Rock - in' and a reelin', Ba'bra Ann,

Ba, ba, ba, Ba'bra Ann.

Chorus 2   *Repeat Chorus 1*

                    F
Verse 2   Played my fav'rite tune, danced with Betty Lou,

                    Tried Peggy Sue, but I knew they wouldn't do.
                        B♭
                    Oh, Ba'bra Ann, Ba'bra Ann, take my hand.
                        F
                    Oh, Ba'bra Ann, Ba'bra Ann, take my hand.
                        C
                    You got me rockin' and a rollin',
                        B♭   **F**
                    Rock - in' and a reelin', Ba'bra Ann,

                    Ba, ba, ba, Ba'bra Ann.

Chorus 3   *Repeat Chorus 1*

Be-Bop-a-Lula

Words and Music by
Tex Davis and Gene Vincent

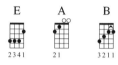

E	A	B
2 3 4 1	2 1	3 2 1 1

Chorus 1

      E
Well, Be-Bop-a-Lula, she's my baby.

Be-Bop-a-Lula, I don't mean maybe.
A
   Be-Bop-a-Lula, she's my baby.
E
   Be-Bop-a-Lula, I don't mean maybe.
B   **A**   **E**
   Be-Bop-a-Lula, she - e - 's my baby doll,

My baby doll, my baby doll.

Verse 1

      E
Well, she's the girl in the red blue jeans.

Ah, she's the queen of all the teens.

Ah, she's the woman that I know.

Ah, she's the woman that loves me so, say.

	A
Chorus 2	Be-Bop-a-Lula, she's my baby.
	E
	Be-Bop-a-Lula, I don't mean maybe.
	B A E
	Be-Bop-a-Lula, she - e - 's my baby doll,
	My baby doll, my baby doll. Let's rock!

Solo 1

E				
A		E		
B	A	E		

Verse 2

         E
Well, now she's the one that's got that beat.

She's the one with the flyin' feet.

She's the one that walks around the store.

She's the one that gets more and more.

Chorus 3   *Repeat Chorus 2*

Solo 2   *Repeat Solo 1*

Chorus 4

         E
Well, Be - Bop-a-Lula, she's my baby.

Be-Bop-a-Lula, I don't mean maybe.
A
  Be-Bop-a-Lula, she's my baby.
E
  Be-Bop-a-Lula, I don't mean maybe.
B   A   E
Be-Bop-a-Lula, she - e - 's my baby doll,

My baby doll, my baby doll.

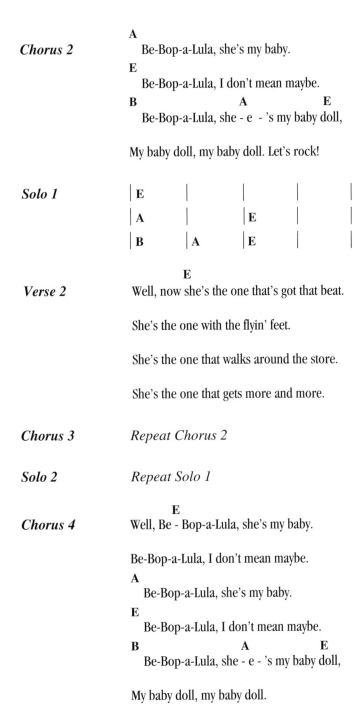

Before You Accuse Me
(Take a Look at Yourself)

Words and Music by
Ellas McDaniels

Melody:

Be - fore you ac-cuse _ me,

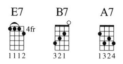

E7   B7   A7

1112   321   1324

| *Intro* | E7 | B7 | E7 |

Verse 1

    E7
Be-fore you accuse me,

A7   **E7**
    Take a look at your-self.

    A7
Be-fore you accuse me,

            E7
Take a look at your-self.

      B7
You said I'm spendin' my money on other women,

A7   **E7**   **B7**
    Been takin' money from someone else.

Verse 2

    E7
I called your mama

A7   **E7**
  'Bout three or four nights a-go.

    A7
I called your mama

          E7
'Bout three or four nights a-go.

    B7
Your mama said, "Son, don't

A7   **E7**   **B7**
Call my daughter no more!"

Verse 3	*Repeat Verse 1*

Guitar Solo 1	*Repeat Verse 1 (Instrumental)*

E7

Verse 4   Come on back home, baby.

      A7   **E7**
      Try my love one more __ time.

         A7
Come on back home, baby.

                   E7
      Try my love one more __ time.

               B7
You know, I don't __ know when to quit you.

      A7   **E7**   **B7**
      I'm gonna lose my mind!   *Robert!*

Guitar Solo 2	*Repeat Verse 1 (Instrumental)*

Verse 5	*Repeat Verse 3*

Outro

E7	A7	E7		
A7		E7		
B7	A7	E7		

Blue Suede Shoes

Words and Music by
Carl Lee Perkins

Melody:

Well, it's a one for the mon- ey,

A   D9   E9

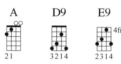

2 1   3 2 1 4   2 3 1 4   4fr

Verse 1

N.C.   A
Well, it's a one for the money,   two for the show.

Three to get ready, now go, cat, go.
         D9   **A**
But don't __ you step on my blue suede shoes.
         E9
Well, you can do anything,
                 A
But stay off of my blue suede shoes.

Verse 2

                 A
Well, you can knock me down, step in my face.

Slander my name all over the place.

Well, do anything that you wanna do.
         N.C.   **A**
But uh-uh, honey, lay off __ of them shoes.
         D9   **A**
And don't __ you step on my blue suede shoes.
         E9
Well, you can do anything,
                 A
But stay off of my blue suede shoes. *Let's go cats!*

Guitar Solo 1

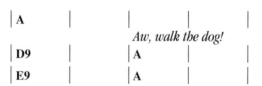

A				
D9		**A**		
E9		**A**		

Aw, walk the dog!

                                    A
Verse 3   Well, you can burn my house, steal my car.

                 Drink my liquor from an old fruit jar.

                 Well, do anything that you wanna do,
                        N.C.   A
                 But uh-uh, honey, lay off __ of my shoes.
                        D9   A
                 And don't __ you step on my blue suede shoes.
                        E9
                 Well, you can do anything,
                                        A
                 But stay off of my blue suede shoes. Rock it!

Guitar Solo 2 | A | | | |
                 | D9 | | A | |
                 | E9 | | A | |

                        A
Verse 4   Well, it's a one for the money, two for the show.
                 N.C.
                 Three to get ready, now go, go, go.
                        D9   A
                 But don't __ you step on my blue suede shoes.
                        E9
                 Well, you can do anything,
                                    A
                 But stay off of my blue suede shoes.

                        A
Outro   Well, it's   blue, blue, blue suede shoes.

                 Blue, blue, blue suede shoes, yeah.
                 D
                   Blue, blue, blue suede shoes, baby.
                 A
                   Blue, blue, blue suede shoes.
                            E9
                 Well, you can do anything
                                    A
                 But stay off of my blue suede shoes.

Bye Bye Love

Words and Music by
Felice Bryant and Boudleaux Bryant

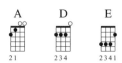

Intro | A | | D | A |

Chorus 1

    D   A
Bye bye, love.

    D   A
Bye bye, happiness.

    D   A
  Hello loneliness.

         E   A
I think I'm gonna cry.

    D   A
Bye bye, love.

    D   A
Bye bye, sweet caress.

    D   A
  Hello emptiness.

         E   A
I feel like I could die.

         E   A
Bye bye, my love, good-bye.

Verse 1

N.C.   **E**
There goes my baby

     A
With someone new.

     E
She sure looks happy,

   A
I sure am blue.

     D
She was my baby

      E
Till he stepped in.

Goodbye to romance

     A
That might have been.

Chorus 2   *Repeat Chorus 1*

Verse 2

        E
I'm through with romance,

     A
I'm through with love.

     E
I'm through with counting

   A
The stars a-bove.

     D
And here's the reason

    E
That I'm so free,

My loving baby

    A
Is through with me.

Chorus 3

D   A
Bye bye, love.

D   A
Bye bye, happiness.

D   A
  Hello loneliness.

          E   A
I think I'm gonna cry.

D   A
Bye bye, love.

D   A
Bye bye, sweet caress.

D   A
  Hello emptiness.

          E   A
I feel like I could die.

          E   A
‖: Bye bye, __ my love, good-bye. :‖   ***Repeat and fade***

Do Wah Diddy Diddy

Words and Music by
Jeff Barry and Ellie Greenwich

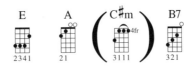

Intro | E | A   E   N.C. |

Verse 1

N.C.
There she was just a walkin' down the street, singin',

E   A   E
"Do wah diddy diddy dum diddy do."

Snappin' her fingers and shufflin' her feet, singin',

                    A   E
"Do wah diddy diddy dum diddy do."

N.C.
She looked good. (Looked good.)

She looked fine. (Looked fine.)

She looked good, she looked fine

And I nearly lost my mind.

THREE CHORD SONGS

Verse 2

        E
Be-fore I knew it she was walkin' next to me, singin',

                A   E
"Do wah diddy diddy dum diddy do."

Holdin' my hand just as natural as can be, singin',

                A   E
"Do wah diddy diddy dum diddy do."

N.C.
We walked on. (Walked on.)

To my door. (My door.)

We walked on to my door,

Then we kissed a little more.

Bridge 1

E
  Whoa,

(C♯m)
I knew we was falling in love.

E
  Yes, I did and so I told her all the things

A   B7
I'd been dreamin' of.

Verse 3

        N.C.
Now we're together nearly ev'ry single day, singin',

E   **A**   **E**
"Do wah diddy diddy dum diddy do."

We're so happy and that's how we're gonna stay, singin',

                  A   **E**
"Do wah diddy diddy dum diddy do."
N.C.
Well, I'm hers. (I'm hers.)

She's mine. (She's mine.)

I'm hers, she's mine.

Wedding bells are gonna chime.

Bridge 2   *Repeat Bridge 1*

Verse 4   *Repeat Verse 3*

             E   **A**   **E**
Outro   ("Do wah diddy diddy dum diddy do.

                  A   **E**
Do wah diddy diddy dum diddy do.

                  A   **E**
Do wah diddy diddy dum diddy do.")

Candle in the Wind

Words and Music by
Elton John and Bernie Taupin

Melody:

Good-bye, Nor - ma Jean. __

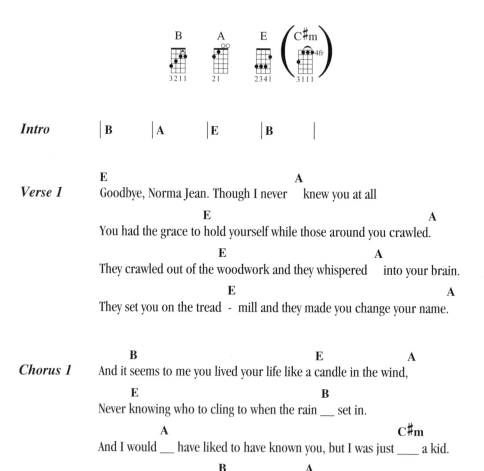

B   A   E   (C#m)

3211   21   2341   3111

Intro | B | A | E | B |

Verse 1
　　　　　E   A
Goodbye, Norma Jean. Though I never   knew you at all
　　　　　　　　　　　　　E   A
You had the grace to hold yourself while those around you crawled.
　　　　　　　　　　　　E   A
They crawled out of the woodwork and they whispered   into your brain.
　　　　　　　　　　　　E   A
They set you on the tread - mill and they made you change your name.

Chorus 1
　　　　　　　B   E   A
And it seems to me you lived your life like a candle in the wind,
　　　　　E   B
Never knowing who to cling to when the rain __ set in.
　　　　　　　　A   C#m
And I would __ have liked to have known you, but I was just ___ a kid.
　　　　　　　　　　　　　B   A
Your candle burned out long before your legend ever did.

Interlude 1 | A | E | | B |
　　　　　　　　 | A | E | B | |

Verse 2

E   A
Loneliness was tough, the toughest role you ever played.

          E   A
Hollywood created a su - perstar and pain was the price you paid.

       E   A
Even when you died, oh, the press __ still hounded you.

         E   A
All the papers had ___ to say was that Marilyn was found in the nude.

Chorus 2 *Repeat Chorus 1*

Interlude 2 *Repeat Interlude 1*

Verse 3

E   A
Goodbye, Norma Jean. Though I never knew you at all

           E   A
You had the grace to hold ___ yourself while those around you crawled.

E   A
Goodbye, Norma Jean, from the young man in the twenty-second row

            E
Who sees you as something more ___ than sexual,

        A
More than just our Marilyn __ Monroe.

Chorus 3

       B   E   A
And it seems to me you lived your life like a candle in the wind,

     E   B
Never knowing who to cling to when the rain __ set in.

      A   C#m
And I would __ have liked to have known you, but I was just ___ a kid.

        B   A   E
Your candle burned out long before your legend ever did.

        B   A   E
Your candle burned out long before your legend ever did.

Cecilia

Words and Music by
Paul Simon

Cel - ia, you're break-ing my heart, _

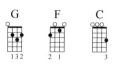

Intro
| N.C.(Percussion) | | | |

Chorus 1

N.C.
Celia, you're breaking my heart,

                                    G
You're shaking my confidence daily.

          F   **C**   **F**   **C**
Oh, Ce - cil - ia, I'm down on my knees,

       F   **C**   **G**
I'm begging you please ___ to come home.

Chorus 2

  C   **F**   **C**
Celia, you're breaking my heart,

       F   **C**   **G**
You're shaking my con - fidence daily.

          F   **C**   **F**   **C**
Oh, Ce - cil - ia, I'm down on my knees,

       F   **C**   **G**
I'm begging you please ___ to come home,

      C
Come on home.

Verse 1

```
        C              F  C
    Making love in the af - ternoon

        F  C  G      C
With Cecilia up in my bed - room,

        F     C
I got up to wash my face.


When I come back to bed,
F       C    G      C
Some - one's taken my place.
```

Chorus 3   *Repeat Chorus 2*

Bridge

```
N.C.                                    G
    Oh, oh, oh, oh, oh, oh, oh, oh, oh, oh, oh, oh, oh, oh.
```

Interlude

```
|C        |F   C  |F   C  |G          |
|F   C    |F   C  |F   C  |G          |
```

Chorus 4

```
        F  C     F       C
Jubi - la - tion, she loves me again,

    F           C        G
I fall on the floor ___ and I laugh - ing.

        F  C     F         C
Jubi - la - tion, she loves me again,

    F           C        G
I fall on the floor ___ and I laugh - ing.
```

Outro

```
          F  C     F      C
||: Oh, oh, oh, oh, oh, oh, oh, oh, oh.

    F          C      G
Oh, oh, oh, oh, oh, oh, oh, oh, oh. :||   Repeat and fade
```

Chantilly Lace

Words and Music by J.P. Richardson

Melody:

Chan - til - ly   lace ___

B7   E   A

Intro   Hello, baby.

Verse 1
```
          B7
          Ya, this is the Big Bopper speakin'.
     E                    B7
     Ha, ha, ha, ha, ha, ha.
                          E
Oh, you sweet thing!
               A
Do I what?
          E
Will I what?
     B7                        E
Oh, baby, you know what I like!
```

Chorus 1
```
                B7
Chantilly lace___ and a pretty face
                E
And a pony tail___ a hangin' down,
                B7
A wiggle in her walk and a giggle in her talk,
E
Make the world go 'round.
               A
There ain't nothin' in the world like a big eyed girl
               E
To make me act so funny, make me spend my money,
               B7
Make me feel real loose like a long necked goose,
          E       N.C.
Like a girl. Oh, baby, that's a what I like.
```

Verse 2

B7
What's that baby?

E   B7
But, but, but,

E   A E
Oh, honey,

 B7   E
But, oh baby, you know what I like!

Chorus 2

Repeat Chorus 1

Verse 3

B7
What's that honey?

E
Pick you up at eight?

     B7 E
And don't be late?

   A   E
But, baby, I ain't got no money, honey!

Ha, ha, ha, ha, ha.
 B7
Oh, alright, honey, you know what I like!

Chorus 3

Repeat Chorus 1

Dizzy Miss Lizzie

Words and Music by
Larry Williams

You make me diz - zy Miss   Liz - zy

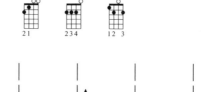

Intro

A				
D		A		
E7	D	A	E7	

Verse 1

                 A
You make me dizzy Miss Lizzy

The way you rock and roll.

                 D
You make me dizzy Miss Lizzy

         A
The way you do the stroll.

       E7
Come on, Miss Lizzy

D   **A**   **E7**
Love me before I get too old.

Verse 2

           A
Come on, give me fever

Put your little hand in mine.

             D   **A**
You make me dizzy miss Lizzy, girl you look so fine.

           E7   **D**   **A E7**
Just a rocking and a rolling, girl I said I wish you were mine.

Interlude 1   *Repeat Intro*

                                         A
Verse 3   You make me dizzy Miss Lizzy

                     When you call my name.
                                         D
                     You make me dizzy Miss Lizzy
                                         A
                     Say you're driving me insane.
                                 E7
                     Come on, Miss Lizzy
                         D   **A**   **E7**
                     I wanna be your loving man.

Interlude 2   *Repeat Intro*

Verse 4   *Repeat Verse 2*

                                         A
Verse 5   You make me dizzy Miss Lizzy

                     When you call my name.
                                         D
                     You make me dizzy Miss Lizzy

                                         A
                     Say you're driving me insane.
                                 E7
                     Come on, Miss Lizzy
                         D   **A**   **D**   **A**
                     I wanna be your loving man.

Donna

Words and Music by
Ritchie Valens

F B♭ C

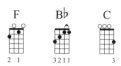

2 1   3 2 1 1   3

Intro

    F   B♭ C
Oh, Donna, oh, Donna.

    F   B♭ C
Oh, Donna, oh, Donna.

Verse 1

      F
  I had a girl,
B♭   C
Donna was her name.

      F
  Since she left me,
     B♭   C
I've never been the same

         F
'Cause I love my girl.
B♭   C   F
Donna, where can you be,
B♭   C
Where can you be?

Verse 2

F
  Now that you're gone,

  B♭   C
I'm left all a-lone.

F
  All by myself

  B♭   C
To wonder and roam

      F
'Cause I love my girl.
B♭   C   F
Donna, where can you be,
B♭   F
Where can you be?

Bridge

      B♭
Oh well, darling,

Now that you're gone,

   F
I don't know what I'll do.

  B♭
Oh, time had all my love

  C
For you, mm.

Verse 3

Repeat Verse 1

Outro

F   B♭ C
Oh, Donna, oh, Donna.
F   B♭ C
Oh, Donna, oh, Donna.
F
Oh.

Dreams

Words and Music by
Stevie Nicks

Now, here you go ___ a - gain. _ You say...

Fmaj7   G   Am

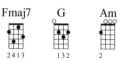

2 4 1 3   1 3 2   2

Intro |Fmaj7 |G |Fmaj7 |G |

Verse 1
     Fmaj7   G
     Now, here you go___ again.

          Fmaj7   G
You say   you want your free - dom.

Fmaj7   G   Fmaj7   G
     Well, who am I___ to keep you down?

Fmaj7   G
     It's only right___ that you should

Fmaj7   G
Play the way you feel___ it.

       Fmaj7   G   Fmaj7
But listen carefully___ to the sound

              G
Of your lone - liness,

Fmaj7   **G**
Like a heartbeat, drives you mad,

        Fmaj7   **G**
In the still - ness of remem-bering

            Fmaj7   **G**   **Fmaj7**   **G**
What you had   and what you lost,

             Fmaj7 **G**   **Fmaj7**   **G**
And what you had   and what you lost.

            Fmaj7   **G**   **Fmaj7**   **G**
Chorus 1   Oh, thunder only hap - pens when it's rain - ing.

       Fmaj7   **G**   **Fmaj7**   **G**
Players only love__ you when they're play - ing.

         Fmaj7   **G**   **Fmaj7**   **G**
Say, women, they will come__ and they will go.

      Fmaj7   **G**   **Fmaj7**   **G**
When the rain washes__ you clean, you'll know.

        Fmaj7
You'll know.

Solo | **Fmaj7** | **G** | **Fmaj7** | |
             | **Am**   **G** | | **Fmaj7** | |

Verse 2

    Fmaj7   G
    Now, here I go__ again.

        Fmaj7   G
I see   the crystal vis - ions.

    Fmaj7   G   Fmaj7   G
    I keep my vis - ions to myself.

    Fmaj7   G
    It's only me__ who wants to

    Fmaj7   G
Wrap around your dreams.

        Fmaj7   G   Fmaj7
And have you any dreams__ you'd like to sell?

                G   Fmaj7   G
Dreams of lone - liness, like a heartbeat, drives you mad,

        Fmaj7   G
In the still - ness of remem-bering

            Fmaj7 G   Fmaj7   G
What you had   and what you lost

            Fmaj7   G   Fmaj7   G
And what you had   and what you lost.

Chorus 2   *Repeat Chorus 1*

Outro

    G   Fmaj7
    You will know.

    G   Fmaj7
Oh,__ you'll know.

Get Back

Words and Music by
John Lennon and Paul McCartney

Melody:

Jo-Jo was a man who thought he was a lon-er,

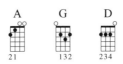

A   G   D
2 1   1 3 2   2 3 4

Intro |A | | | G   D |

Verse 1
A
Jo-Jo was a man who thought he was a loner,

D   **A**
But he knew it couldn't last.

Jo-Jo left his home in Tucson, Arizona

D   **A**
For some California grass.

Chorus 1
          A
Get back, get back,

          D   **A**   **G**   **D**
Get back to where you once belonged.

          A
Get back, get back,

          D   **A**
Get back to where you once belonged.

Get back, Jo-Jo.

Solo 1　　　　　‖: A　　|　　　|D　　　|A　G　D :‖

Chorus 2
　　　　　　　　A
　　　　　　Get back, get back,
　　　　　　　　D　　　　　　　　　A　　G　　D
　　　　　　Get back to where you once belonged.
　　　　　　　　A
　　　　　　Get back, get back,
　　　　　　　　D　　　　　　　　　A
　　　　　　Get back to where you once belonged.
　　　　　　　　　A
　　　　　　Get back, Jo-Jo.

Solo 2　　　　　*Repeat Solo 1*

Verse 2
　　　　　　　　A
　　　　　　Sweet Loretta Martin though she was a woman,
　　　　　　　　D　　　　　　A
　　　　　　But she was another man.

　　　　　　All the girls around her say she's got it coming
　　　　　　　　D　　　　　　　A
　　　　　　But she gets it while she can.

Chorus 3

    A
Get back, get back,

    D   **A**   **G**   **D**
Get back to where you once belonged.

    A
Get back, get back,

    D   **A**
Get back to where you once belonged.

Get back, Loretta.

Solo 3   *Repeat Solo 1*

    A
Chorus 4   Get back, get back,

    D   **A**   **G**   **D**
Get back to where you once belonged.

    A
Get back, get back,

    D
Get back to where you once belonged.   Ooh.

‖: **A** | |**D** |**A**   **G**   **D** :‖ *Repeat and fade*
        Get back.

The First Cut Is the Deepest

Words and Music by
Cat Stevens

I would have giv-en you all ___ of my heart, _

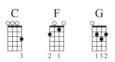

Intro   ‖: C   F G | | C   F G | :‖

Verse 1

                C   G   F G
I would have given you all ___ of my heart,

                C   G   F G
But there's someone who's torn it apart.

              C   G   F
And she's taken just all ___ that I had.

       G   C   G   F
But, if you want, I'll   try to love again. ___ Oh, babe

G   C   F   G
Baby, I'll try ___ to love a - gain, but I know.

Chorus 1

       C   G   F
    The first cut is the deep - est.

G   C   G   F   G
Baby, I know   the first cut is the deep - est.

             C   G   F   G
Cause when it comes to bein' lucky she's cursed.

        C   F   G
When it comes to lovin' me, she's worse.

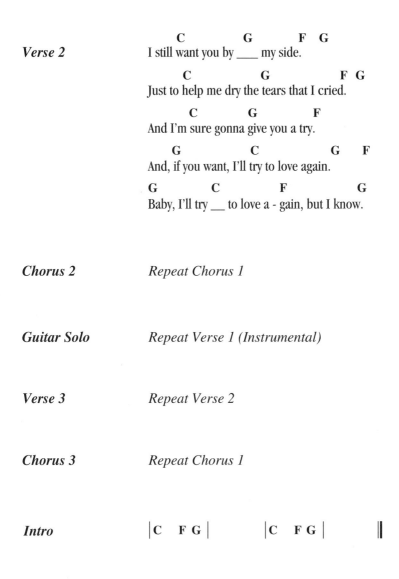

Verse 2

```
        C          G        F  G
I still want you by ___ my side.
            C          G          F  G
Just to help me dry the tears that I cried.
            C       G        F
And I'm sure gonna give you a try.
        G          C          G    F
And, if you want, I'll try to love again.
G          C         F           G
Baby, I'll try __ to love a - gain, but I know.
```

Chorus 2   *Repeat Chorus 1*

Guitar Solo   *Repeat Verse 1 (Instrumental)*

Verse 3   *Repeat Verse 2*

Chorus 3   *Repeat Chorus 1*

Intro | C   F G | | C   F G | ‖

409

Words and Music by
Brian Wilson, Gary Usher and Mike Love

Melody:

She's real fine, my four - o - nine. _

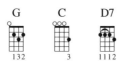

G	C	D7
1 3 2	3	1 1 1 2

Intro

N.C.
She's real fine, my four-o-nine.

She's real fine, my four-o-nine,

　　　G
My four-o-nine.

Verse 1

G
Well, I saved my pennies and I saved my dimes.

(Giddy-up, giddy-up four-o-nine.)
C
For I knew there would be a time
G
(Giddy-up, giddy-up four-o-nine.)
　　D7　　　　　　　**C**　　　　　**G**
When I would buy a brand ___ new four-o-nine.

Chorus 1

G
Giddy-up, giddy-up, giddy-up four-o-nine.

C
Giddy-up four-o-nine.

G
Giddy-up four-o-nine.

Giddy-up four-o...

D7
Nothing can catch her,

C   G
Nothing can touch my four-o-nine, four-o-nine.

Guitar Solo

G
(Oo, giddy-up, giddy-up.

Oo, giddy-up, giddy-up.

C
Oo, giddy-up, giddy-up.

G   D7   C   G
Oo, giddy-up, giddy-up.)

Verse 2

G
When I take her to the drag, she really shines.

(Giddy-up, giddy-up four-o-nine.)

C
She always turns in the fastest time.

G
(Giddy-up, giddy-up four-o-nine.)

D7   C   G
My four-speed, dual quad, posi-traction four-o-nine.

Chorus 2   *Repeat Chorus 1*

Outro

G
‖: Giddy-up four-o-nine.   :‖ *Repeat and fade*

Give Me One Reason

Words and Music by
Tracy Chapman

Melody:

Give me one   rea-son to   stay   here __

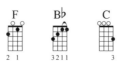

F   Bb   C

2 1   3211   3

Intro | F | Bb   C | F | | |
           | Bb | C | F | | |
           | C | Bb | F | | |

                F
Verse 1   Give me one reason to stay here

             Bb   C   F
                 And I'll__ turn right back a-round.

             Bb
             Give me one reason to stay here

                         C   F
             And I'll__ turn right back a-round.

                          C
             Said I don't wanna leave you lonely,

             Bb   F
                 You got to make me change my mind.

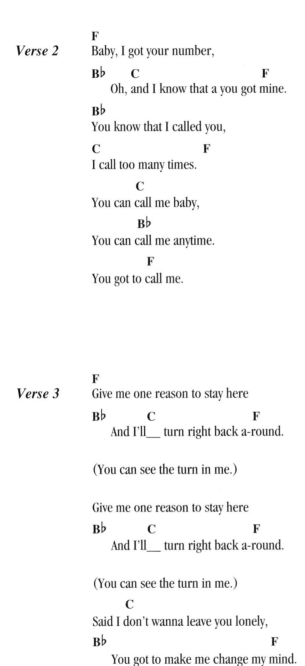

Verse 2

F
Baby, I got your number,

B♭   C   F
    Oh, and I know that a you got mine.

B♭
You know that I called you,

C   F
I call too many times.

        C
You can call me baby,

        B♭
You can call me anytime.

           F
You got to call me.

Verse 3

F
Give me one reason to stay here

B♭   C   F
    And I'll___ turn right back a-round.

(You can see the turn in me.)

Give me one reason to stay here

B♭   C   F
    And I'll___ turn right back a-round.

(You can see the turn in me.)

        C
Said I don't wanna leave you lonely,

B♭   F
    You got to make me change my mind.

Verse 4

            F
I don't want no one to squeeze me,

B♭   **C**   **F**
   They might take away my life.

I don't want no one to squeeze me,

B♭   **C**   **F**
   They might take away my life.

      C
I just want someone to hold me,

B♭   **F**
   Oh, and rock me through the night.

Interlude   *Repeat Verse 4 (Instrumental)*

Verse 5

            F
This youthful heart can love you,

B♭   **C**   **F**
   Yes, and give you what you need.

         B♭
I said this youthful heart can love you,

C   **F**
   Ho, and give you what you need.

       C
But I'm too old to go chasin' you around,

B♭   **F**
   Wastin' my precious energy.

		F
Verse 6		Give me one reason to stay here,

Bb   C   F
   Yes, now turn right back a-round.

(Around. You can see the turn in me.)

Give me one reason to stay here,
Bb   C   F
   Oh, I'll turn right back a-round.

(You can see the turn in me.)
       C
Said I don't wanna leave you lonely,
Bb   F
   You got to make me change my mind.

		F
Verse 7		Baby, just give me one reason,

Bb   C   F
   Oh, give me just one reason why.
Bb
Baby, just give me one reason,
C   F
   Oh, give me just one reason why,

I should stay.
       C
Said I told you that I loved you,
Bb N.C.   F
   And there ain't no more to say.

Hang On Sloopy

Words and Music by
Wes Farrell and Bert Russell

Hang _____ on, Sloo-py, Sloo-py, hang on. _____

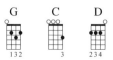

Intro | N.C.(G) (C) | (D) (C) |

Chorus 1

    G   C   D   C   G C D C
Hang _____ on Sloopy, Sloopy hang on.

    G   C   D   C   G C D C
Hang _____ on Sloopy, Sloopy hang on.

Verse 1

    G   C   D   C   G C D C
Sloopy lives _____ in a very bad _____ part of town.

      G   C   D   C   G C D C
And ev'rybod - y here _____ tries to put my Sloopy down.

    G   C   D   C   G C D C
Sloopy, I _____ don't care _____ what your Daddy do.

      G   C   D   C   G C D
'Cause you know, Sloopy, girl, _____ I'm in love with you.

And so I say now,

Chorus 2	*Repeat Chorus 1*

Verse 2

<pre>
G   C   D   C   G C D C
Sloopy wears a red dress, yeah, ___ as old as the hills.
        G   C   D
But when Sloopy wears that red dress, yeah,
          C   G   C D C
You know, it gives me the chills.
G   C   D   C   G   C D C
Sloopy when I see you walk - in', walkin, down the street
        G   C   D   C   G C D
I say, "Don't worry, Sloopy, girl, ___ you be - long to me."
</pre>

And so I say now,

Chorus 3	*Repeat Chorus 1*

Guitar Solo   ‖:N.C.(G) (C) |(D)   (C)   :‖ *Play 4 times*

Interlude   ‖:N.C.(G) (C) |(D)   (C)   :‖

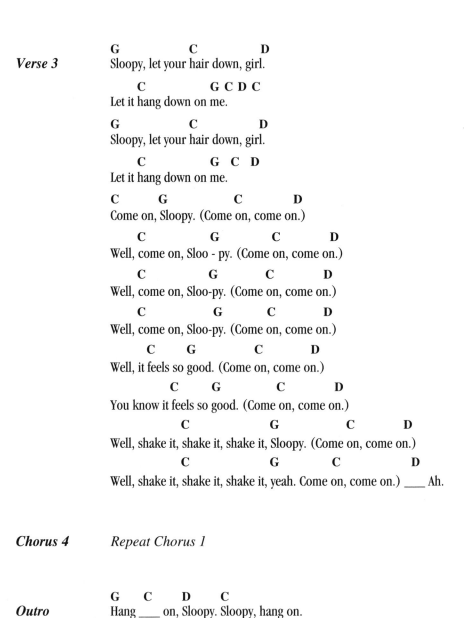

Verse 3

G   C   D
Sloopy, let your hair down, girl.

     C   G C D C
Let it hang down on me.

G   C   D
Sloopy, let your hair down, girl.

     C   G C D
Let it hang down on me.

C   G   C   D
Come on, Sloopy. (Come on, come on.)

    C   G   C   D
Well, come on, Sloo - py. (Come on, come on.)

    C   G   C   D
Well, come on, Sloo-py. (Come on, come on.)

    C   G   C   D
Well, come on, Sloo-py. (Come on, come on.)

     C G   C   D
Well, it feels so good. (Come on, come on.)

         C   G   C   D
You know it feels so good. (Come on, come on.)

              C   G   C   D
Well, shake it, shake it, shake it, Sloopy. (Come on, come on.)

              C   G   C   D
Well, shake it, shake it, shake it, yeah. Come on, come on.) ___ Ah.

Chorus 4   *Repeat Chorus 1*

Outro

G   C   D   C
Hang ___ on, Sloopy. Sloopy, hang on.

| G   C | D   C | G   ‖

Kiss

Words and Music by
Prince

You don't have to be   beau - ti - ful

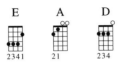

Intro | E   N.C. | A | | |
                Uh.

Verse 1   A N.C.   A
                You don't have to be beautiful to turn me on.

                I just need your body, baby, from dusk 'till dawn.

                                         D
                You don't need ex - perience, ah, to turn me out, ah.

                                         A
                You just leave it all up to me, ah.

                I'm gonna show you what it's all about, now.

Chorus 1

              E
You don't have to be rich to be my girl.

                     D
You don't have to be cool ____ to rule my world.

                  E
Ain't no particular sign ____ I'm more compatible with.

          D   E N.C.
I just want your extra time and your   kiss.

Interlude 1 | A | | |

               Ah,   Oh, oh.

Verse 2

A N.C.   A
    You got to not talk dirty, babe, uh, if you wanna impress me.

You can't be too flirty, mama, I know how to undress me, yeah.

              D
I want to be your fantasy. Maybe you could be mine.

              A
You just leave it all up to me and we can have a good time, uh.

Chorus 2

              E
Don't have to be rich to be my girl.

                   D
You don't have to be cool ____ to rule my world.

                  E
Ain't no particular sign ____ I'm more compatible with.

          D   E N.C.
I just want your extra time and your   kiss.

Interlude 2 | **A** | | | **N.C.** |
Yes.   Oh, ah.   I _____think I wanna dance.

Guitar Solo | **A** | | |
Uh.   Ah, whew.

| | | | |
Uh, I got to, got   to,   oh.   Little girl, Wendy's parade.

| **D** | | | |
Got to, got to, got

| **A** | | | **N.C.** |
To.   Woman, not

A

Verse 3   Girls, rule my world, I said they rule my world.

Act your age, mama, not your shoe size.

Maybe we could do the twirl.

D
You don't have to watch Dynasty to have an attitude.

A
Uh. You just leave it all up to me.

My love will be your food. Yeah.

Chorus 3   *Repeat Chorus 1*

Hound Dog

Words and Music by
Jerry Leiber and Mike Stoller

You ain't noth-in' but a hound dog - a,...

C   F7   G7

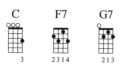

3   2314   213

Chorus 1

               C
You ain't nothin' but a hound dog a,

C-cryin' all the time.

           F7
You ain't nothin' but a hound dog a,

   C
Cryin' all the time.

    G7
Well, you ain't never caught a rabbit

  F7   **N.C.**
And you ain't no friend of mine.

Verse 1

               C
Well, they said you was high - classed.

Well, that was just a lie.

         F7
Yeah, they said you was high-class.

      C
Well, that was just a lie.

    G7
Well, you ain't never caught a rabbit

  F7   **N.C.**
And you ain't no friend of mine.

Chorus 2   *Repeat Chorus 1*

Solo 1

C				
F7		C		
G7	F7	C		

Verse 2   *Repeat Verse 1*

Solo 2   *Repeat Solo 1*

Verse 3   *Repeat Verse 1*

Chorus 3

         C
You ain't nothin' but a hound dog a,

C-cryin' all the time.

         F
You ain't nothin' but a hound dog a,

  C
Cryin' all the time.

     G7   **N.C.**
Well, you ain't never caught a rab-bit;

       C
You ain't no friend of mine.

You ain't nothin' but a hound dog.

The House Is Rockin'

Written by Stevie Ray Vaughan and
Doyle Bramhall

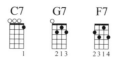

Intro ‖: C7 | | | :‖

Chorus 1

C7
Well, the house is a rockin', but don't bother knockin'.

Yeah, the house is a rockin', but don't bother knockin'.

  G7   C7
If the house is a rockin', don't bother, come on in.

Verse 1

C7
Kick off your shoes, start losin' the blues.

This old house ain't got nothin' to lose.

  F7   C7
Seen it all for years, a start spreadin' the news.

  G7   C7
We got room on the floor, come on, baby, shake somethin' loose!

Chorus 2 *Repeat Chorus 1*

Piano Solo *Repeat Verse 1 (Instrumental)*

Guitar Solo

	C7								
	F7			C7					
	G7								
	C7								

Chorus 2   *Repeat Chorus 1*

Verse 2
C7
Walkin' up the street, you can hear the sound

Of some bad honky tonkers really layin' it down.
                 F7   C7
They've seen it all for years, they got nothin' to lose.
        G7   C7
So get out on the floor, shimmy till you shake somethin' loose!

Chorus 3   *Repeat Chorus 1*

Outro
        G7   C7
I said the house is a rockin', don't bother, come on in.

I Fought the Law

Words and Music by
Sonny Curtis

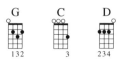

Intro

|G | |G |C   D |
|G |D G D G |

Verse 1

    G   C   G
A breakin' rocks in the   hot sun.

    G   C   G
I fought the law and the   law won.

                      D   G
I fought the law and the   law won.

|C   D |G |D G D G |

Verse 2

    G   C   G
I miss my baby and the   good fun.

    G   C   G
I fought the law and the   law won.

                      D   G
I fought the law and the   law won.

|C   D |G |D G D G |

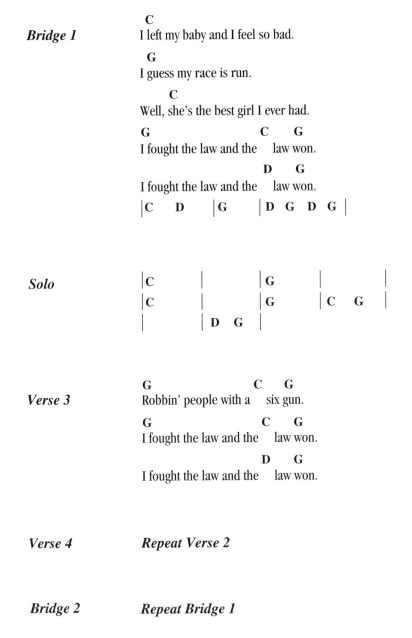

Bridge 1

     C
I left my baby and I feel so bad.

     G
I guess my race is run.

       C
Well, she's the best girl I ever had.

G   C   G
I fought the law and the   law won.

                    D   G
I fought the law and the   law won.

| C   D | G | D G D G |

Solo

C		G	
C		G	C G
	D G

Verse 3

G   C   G
Robbin' people with a   six gun.

G   C   G
I fought the law and the law won.

                    D   G
I fought the law and the law won.

Verse 4   **Repeat Verse 2**

Bridge 2   **Repeat Bridge 1**

Kansas City

Words and Music by
Jerry Leiber and Mike Stoller

G7   F7   C

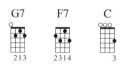

Intro |G7 |F7 |C | |

Verse 1
                    C
I'm goin' to   Kansas City,

Kansas City here I come.
              F7
I'm goin' to   Kansas City,
                    C
Kansas City here I come.
           G7
They got a crazy way of lovin' there and
F7   **C**
I'm gonna get me some.

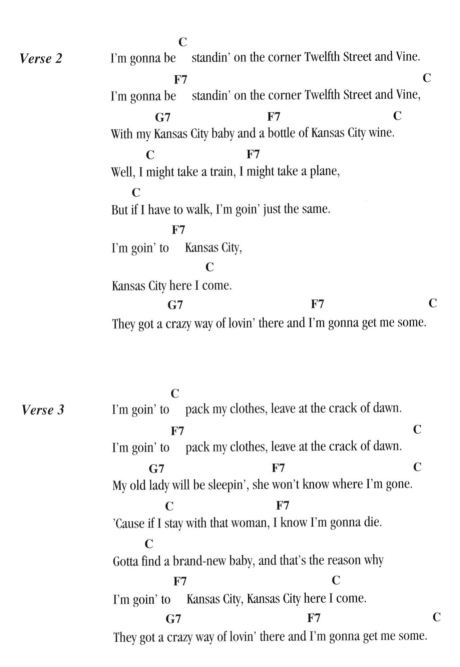

Verse 2

                                C

I'm gonna be   standin' on the corner Twelfth Street and Vine.

                       F7   C

I'm gonna be   standin' on the corner Twelfth Street and Vine,

           G7   F7   C

With my Kansas City baby and a bottle of Kansas City wine.

               C   F7

Well, I might take a train, I might take a plane,

               C

But if I have to walk, I'm goin' just the same.

                   F7

I'm goin' to   Kansas City,

                       C

Kansas City here I come.

           G7   F7   C

They got a crazy way of lovin' there and I'm gonna get me some.

Verse 3

                         C

I'm goin' to   pack my clothes, leave at the crack of dawn.

                     F7   C

I'm goin' to   pack my clothes, leave at the crack of dawn.

           G7   F7   C

My old lady will be sleepin', she won't know where I'm gone.

                     C   F7

'Cause if I stay with that woman, I know I'm gonna die.

               C

Gotta find a brand-new baby, and that's the reason why

                    F7   C

I'm goin' to   Kansas City, Kansas City here I come.

           G7   F7   C

They got a crazy way of lovin' there and I'm gonna get me some.

La Bamba

By Ritchie Valens

Melody:

Pa - ra bai - lar La Bam - ba.

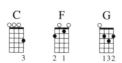

C   F   G

Intro | C   F G | | C   F | G

Verse 1

N.C.   C   F   G
Para bailar La Bam - ba.

                        C   F   G
Para bailar La Bam - ba, se nece-sita

             C   F   G
Un poca de gracia.

             C   F   G
Una poca de gracia para mi para ti

             C   F   G
Y arriba, arri - ba,

                   C   F   G
Y arriba, arri - ba, por ti se re,

       C   F   G
Por ti se re, por ti se re.

                 C   F   G
Yo no soy mari-nero.

                   C   F   G
You no soy mari-nero, soy capi-tan,

          C   F   G
Soy capitan,___ soy capi-tan.

Chorus 1

```
C   F  G
```
Bam-ba, bamba.
```
C   F  G
```
Bam-ba, bamba.
```
C   F  G
```
Bam-ba, Bamba.
```
C   F
```
Bam-ba.

Verse 2

```
G N.C.           C   F  G
```
  Para bailar La Bam - ba.
```
                 C     F     G
```
Para bailar La Bam - ba, se nece-sita
```
              C    F  G
```
Un poca de gracia.
```
             C         F      G
```
Una poca de gracia para mi para ti
```
              C
```
Y arriba, arri - ba.

Solo

‖: C   F   G | :‖   *Play 7 times*

Verse 3

```
              C    F  G
```
Para bailar La Bam - ba.
```
              C     F     G
```
Para bailar La Bam - ba, se nece-sita
```
             C    F  G
```
Un poca de gracia.
```
             C         F      G
```
Una poca de gracia para mi para ti
```
            C    F  G
```
Y arriba, arri - ba,
```
              C       F   G
```
Y arriba, arri - ba, por ti se re,
```
          C     F     G
```
Por ti se re, por ti se re.

Outro

```
C   F  G
```
‖: Bam-ba, bamba.
```
C   F  G
```
Bam-ba, bamba. :‖   *Repeat and fade*

Lay Down Sally

Words and Music by Eric Clapton,
Marcy Levy and George Terry

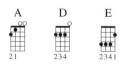

A	D	E

Intro ‖: A | | :‖ **Play 4 times**

Verse 1

A
There is nothing that is wrong

                  D
In wanting you to stay here with me.

  A
I know you've got somewhere to go,

                        D
But won't you make yourself at home and stay with me?

           E
And don't you ever leave.

Chorus 1

A
Lay down, Sally,

   D
And rest you in my arms.

E   A
Don't you think you want someone to talk __ to?

Lay down Sally,

   D
No need to leave so soon.

E
I've been trying all night long

    A
Just to talk with you.

Verse 2

                  A
The sun ain't nearly on the rise,

                                         D
And we still got the moon and stars a-bove.

A
Underneath the velvet skies,

Love is all that matters;

                D
Won't you stay with me?

                     E
And don't you ever leave.

Chorus 2   *Repeat Chorus 1*

Guitar Solo   ‖: A | | | :‖ *Play 8 times*

	A
Verse 3	I long to see the morning light

                          D

Coloring your face so dreami-ly.

  A

So don't you go and say goodbye.

You can lay your worries down

  D

And stay with me.

      E

And don't you ever leave.

  A

Chorus 3   Lay down, Sally,

    D

And rest you in my arms.

E   **A**

Don't you think you want someone to talk __ to?

Lay down Sally,

      D

There's no need to leave so soon.

E   **A**

I've been trying all night long just to talk with you.

Chorus 4   *Repeat Chorus 3*

Outro   ‖: A | | :‖ *Repeat and fade*

Leaving on a Jet Plane

Words and Music by
John Denver

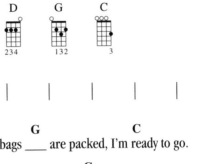

Intro

|D | | | | | |

Verse 1

                          G   C
All my bags ____ are packed, I'm ready to go.

G   C
I'm standing here out - side your door,

G   C   D
I hate to wake you up to say good - bye.

                      G   C
But the dawn is breakin', it's early morn,

                   G   C
The taxi's waitin', he's blowin' his horn,

G   C   D
    Already I'm so lonesome I could die.

Chorus 1

                      G   C
So kiss me and smile for me,

G   C
Tell me that you'll wait for me,

G   C   D
Hold me like you'll never let me go.

                      G   C
'Cause I'm leavin' on a jet plane,

G   C
    Don't know when I'll ____ be back again.

G   C   D
    Oh, babe, I hate ____ to go.

Verse 2

```
          G              C
There's so many times I let you down,
      G                 C
So ___ many times I've ___ played around,
   G              C              D
   But I tell you now   they don't mean ___ a thing.
        G           C
Ev'ry place I go I'll think of you,
      G           C
Ev'ry song I sing I'll sing for you,
        G           C              D
When I come back I'll bring your wedding ___ ring.
```

Chorus 2   *Repeat Chorus 1*

Verse 3

```
   G              C
   Now the time ___ has come to leave you,
   G              C
   One more time ___ let me kiss you,
   G              C      D
   Then close your eyes, ___ I'll ___ be on my way.
   G                 C
Dream about the days ___ to come
     G                    C
When I won't have to leave ___ alone,
     G           C              D
A - bout the times   I won't have ___ to say...
```

Chorus 3

        G   C
Oh, kiss me and smile for me,

G   C
Tell me that you'll wait for me,

G   C   D
Hold me like you'll___ never let me go.

           G   C
'Cause I'm leavin' on a jet plane,

G   C
   Don't know when I'll ___ be back again.

G   C   D
   Oh, babe, I hate to go.

Outro

          G   C   G
But I'm leavin' on a jet plane,

                   C   G
Don't know when I'll ___ be back again,

   C   D   G
Oh, babe, I hate to go.

Lively Up Yourself

Words and Music by
Bob Marley

You're gon - na live - ly up your - self, ___

D   G

234   132

Intro

|N.C.(D) |(G) |(D) | | |
| |(G) |(D) | | |

Chorus 1

        D   **G**   **D   G**
You're gonna lively up yourself, ___ and don't be no drag.

    D   **G**   **D**   **G**
You lively up yourself, ___ oh, reggae is a-nother bag.

    D   **G**   **D   G**
You lively up yourself, ___ and don't say no.

       D   **G**   **D**
You're gonna lively up yourself, ___ 'cause I said so.

   G
Hear what you gonna do.

Verse 1

      D   **G**   **D**   **G**
You rock so you rock so,   like you never did before. Yeah.

    D   **G D**   **G**
You dip so you dip so,   dip through my door.

    D   **G**   **D**   **G**
You come so you come so.   Oh, ___ yeah.

    D   **G**   **D   G**
You skank so you skank so,   be alive to - day.

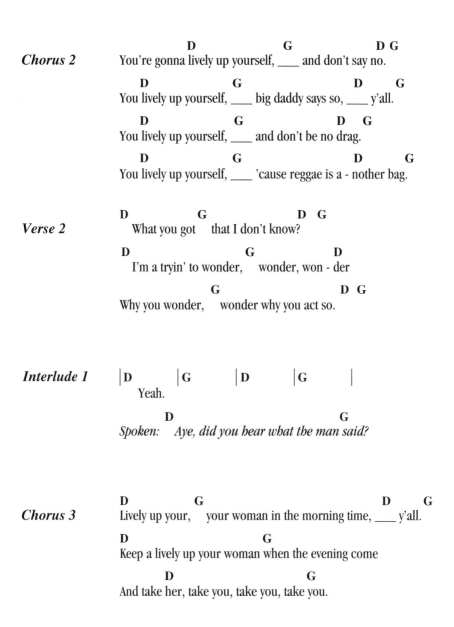

Chorus 2

                        D   G   D G

You're gonna lively up yourself, ___ and don't say no.

      D   G   D   G

You lively up yourself, ___ big daddy says so, ___ y'all.

      D   G   D   G

You lively up yourself, ___ and don't be no drag.

      D   G   D   G

You lively up yourself, ___ 'cause reggae is a - nother bag.

Verse 2

D   G   D G

 What you got   that I don't know?

D   G   D

 I'm a tryin' to wonder,   wonder, won - der

                  G   D G

Why you wonder,   wonder why you act so.

Interlude 1

|D |G |D |G |

 Yeah.

                D   G

Spoken: *Aye, did you hear what the man said?*

Chorus 3

D   G   D   G

Lively up your,   your woman in the morning time, ___ y'all.

D   G

Keep a lively up your woman when the evening come

           D   G

And take her, take you, take you, take you.

Interlude 2

      D   G   D   G

Come on, baby, 'cause I, I wanna be lively myself, y'all.

‖: D |G |D |G   :‖ *Play 7 times*

Chorus 4

    D   G   D   G

Lively up yourself.

    D   G   D   G

Lively up yourself.

Sax Solo

            D   G

You're gonna rock so you rock so.

‖: D |G   :‖ *Play 7 times*

Verse 3

    D   G D G

You rock so, you rock so.

    D   G D G

You dip so, you dip so.

    D   G   D   G

You skank so you skank so,   and don't be no drag.

    D   G   D   G

You come so, you come so.   Oh, reggae is a - nother bag.

                          D   G

Spoken: Get what you get in that bag.

Outro

    D   G   D G

What you got in that other bag you got hangin' there?

    D   G

What you say you got?

D G   D G   D G

I don't believe you.   **Fade out**

Mellow Yellow

Words and Music by
Donovan Leitch

I'm   just   mad a-bout Saf - fron.

D5   G5   A5

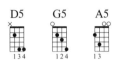

Intro

| N.C.(Drums) | | | |

Verse 1

D5   G5
I'm just mad about Saf - fron.

    D5   A5
Uh, Saffron's mad about me.

G5
I'm, uh, just mad about Saffron.

A5
She's just mad about me.

Chorus 1

                                D5   G5
They call me Mellow Yellow. *Whispered: (Quite rightly.)*

        A5   D5   G5
They call me Mellow Yellow. *(Quite rightly.)*

        A5   D5   G5   A5
They call me Mellow Yellow.

Verse 2

D5   G5
I'm just mad about Four - teen.

    D5   A5
Uh, Fourteen's mad about me.

G5
I'm, buh, just, uh, mad about, uh, Fourteen.

    A5
Uh, she's just mad about me.

Chorus 2

                                  D5   **G5**
They call me Mellow Yellow.

          A5   **D5**   **G5**
They call me Mellow Yellow. *(Quite rightly.)*

          A5   **D5**   **G5** **A5**
They call me Mellow Yellow.

Verse 3

D5   **G5**
Born ah, high forever to ___ fly.

D5   **A5**
Uh, wind, uh, velocity: nil.

G5
Born, ah, high forever to fly,

A5
If you want, your cup I will fill.

Chorus 3

                                  D5   **G5**
They call me Mellow Yellow. *Whispered: (Quite rightly.)*

          A5   **D5**   **G5**
They call me Mellow Yellow. *(Quite rightly.)*

          A5   **D5**   **G5**
They call me Mellow Yellow.

A5
  So mellow, yellow fellow.

Horn Solo

Repeat Verse 1 (Instrumental)

D5	**G5**	**A5**	**D5**	**G5**	**A5**	
D5	**G5** $\frac{2}{4}$		$\frac{4}{4}$ **A5**			

Verse 4

D5   **G5**
Electrical ba - nana

  D5   **A5**
Is gonna be a sudden craze.

G5   **A5**
Electrical banana is bound to be the very next phase.

Chorus 4   *Repeat Chorus 1*

Verse 5

D5   **G5**
Eh, Saffron.   Eh, yeah.

D5   **A5**
I'm just mad about her.

    G5
Well, I'm, huh, just, uh, mad about, uh, Saffron.

A5
She's just mad about me.

Chorus 5

               D5   **G5**
They call me Mellow Yellow. *(Quite rightly.)*

    A5   **D5**   **G5**
They call me Mellow Yellow. *(Quite rightly.)*

    A5   **D5**   **G5 A5**
(They call me …) Oh, so ___ yellow.

D5   **G5 A5**   **D5**
Oh, ___ so mellow.   Oh, so mellow. *Fade out*

Long Tall Sally

Words and Music by Enotris Johnson,
Richard Penniman and Robert Blackwell

Gon-na tell Aunt Mar - y 'bout Un-cleJohn.

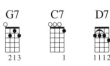

Verse 1

G7 N.C.   G7 N.C.
Gonna tell Aunt Mary 'bout Uncle John.

G7 N.C.
Said he had the mis'ry, but he got a lot of fun.

C7
Oh, ba - by,

      G7
Yeah now, ba - by.

D7   C7   G7
Woo, ba - by,   some fun tonight.

Verse 2

G7 N.C.   G7 N.C.
Well, I saw Uncle John with blond headed Sally.

G7 N.C.
He saw Aunt Mary comin' and he ducked back in the alley.

C7
Oh, ba - by,

     G7
Yeah now, ba - by.

D7
Woo, ba - by,

C7   G7
Have some fun tonight. ___ Ah!

Solo 1

G7					
C7		G7			
D7	C7	G7			

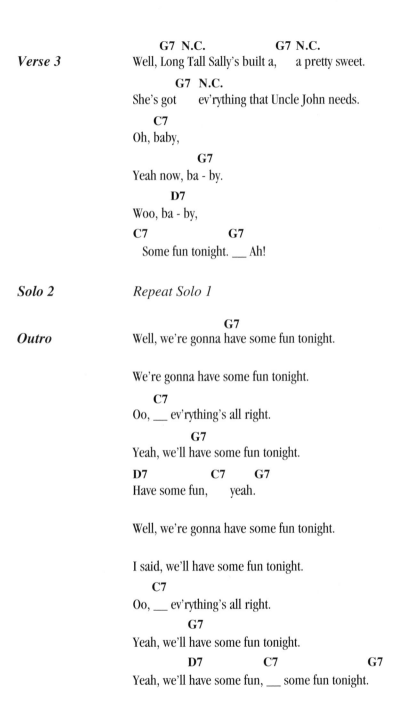

Verse 3

       G7 N.C.   **G7 N.C.**
Well, Long Tall Sally's built a,   a pretty sweet.

       G7 N.C.
She's got   ev'rything that Uncle John needs.

  C7
Oh, baby,

      G7
Yeah now, ba - by.

     D7
Woo, ba - by,

C7   **G7**
  Some fun tonight. __ Ah!

Solo 2   *Repeat Solo 1*

         G7
Outro   Well, we're gonna have some fun tonight.

We're gonna have some fun tonight.

  C7
Oo, __ ev'rything's all right.

     G7
Yeah, we'll have some fun tonight.

D7   **C7**   **G7**
Have some fun,   yeah.

Well, we're gonna have some fun tonight.

I said, we'll have some fun tonight.

  C7
Oo, __ ev'rything's all right.

    G7
Yeah, we'll have some fun tonight.

      D7   **C7**   **G7**
Yeah, we'll have some fun, __ some fun tonight.

Love Me Do

Words and Music by John Lennon
and Paul McCartney

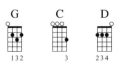

Intro | G | C | G | C | G | C | G | | |

Chorus 1

      G   C
Love, love me do.

        G   C
You know I love you.

       G   C
I'll always be true.

So please,

N.C.   G   C   G   C
Love me do. ____ Oh, love me do.

Chorus 2   *Repeat Chorus 1*

Bridge

     D
Someone to love,

    C   G
Somebody new.

     D
Someone to love,

    C   G
Someone like you.

Chorus 3

G   C
Love, love me do.

  G   C
You know I love you.

  G   C
I'll always be true.

So please,

N.C. G C G
Love me do. ____ Oh, love me do.

Solo

‖: D | | C | G :‖

| | | | D |

Chorus 4

G   C
Love, love me do.

  G   C
You know I love you.

  G   C
I'll always be true.

So please,

N.C. G C G   C
Love me do. ____ Oh, love me do.

   G   C
‖: Yeah, love me do.

  G   C
Oh, love me do. :‖ *Repeat and fade*

Me and Bobby McGee

Words and Music by
Kris Kristofferson and Fred Foster

Melody:

Bust-ed   flat ___   in Bat - on Rouge,

G   C   D

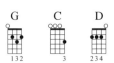

1 3 2   3   2 3 4

Intro | G | C | G   C | G |

Verse 1
G
Busted flat in Baton Rouge, waitin' for a train,

                                        D
When I was feelin' nearly faded as my ___ jeans.

Bobby thumbed a diesel down just before it rained;

                           G   C   G
They rode us all the way to New Or-leans.

Verse 2
G
I pulled my harpoon out of my dirty red bandanna,

                                              C
I was playin' soft while Bob - by sang the blues, ___ yeah.

                           G
Windshield wipers slap in time, I was holdin' Bobby's hand in mine.

D
We sang ev'ry song that driver knew.

Chorus 1

    C   G
Freedom's just another word for ___ nothin' left to lose.

    D   G
Nothin', don't mean nothin', hon', if it ain't free, no, no,

     C   G
If feelin' good was easy, Lord, ___ when he sang the blues,

                D
You know feelin' good was good enough for me,

                                   G
Good enough for me and my Bobby Mc-Gee.

Verse 3

                    G
From the Kentucky coal mines to the California sun,

                               D
Hey, Bobby shared the secrets of my ___ soul.

Through all kinds of weather, through ev'rything that we've done, yeah,

                              G
Bobby, baby, helped me from the whole ___ world.

Verse 4

           G
One day up near Salinas, Lord, I let him slip away.

                          C
He's lookin' for that home and I hope he finds it.

                           G
But I'd trade all of my tomorrows for one single yesterday

        D
To be holdin' Bobby's body next to mine.

Chorus 2

    C   G
Freedom's just another word for ___ nothin' left to lose.

    D
Nothin', that's all that Bobby left me, yeah.

       C   G
But if feelin' good was easy, Lord, ___ when he sang the blues, hey,

    D
Feelin' good was good enough for me, mm, hmm,

                                 G
Good enough for me and my Bobby Mc-Gee.

Mony, Mony

Words and Music by Bobby Bloom,
Tommy James, Ritchie Cordell and Bo Gentry

Melody:

Here ___ she comes now say-ing,

F B♭ C

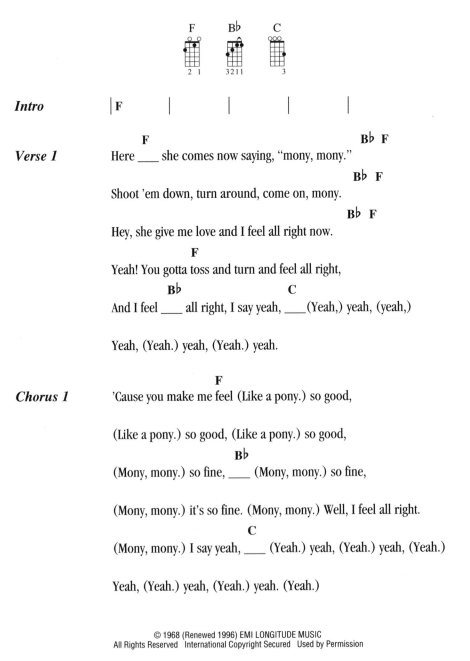

Intro | F | | | |

Verse 1
          F   B♭ F

Here ___ she comes now saying, "mony, mony."

                                        B♭ F

Shoot 'em down, turn around, come on, mony.

                                        B♭ F

Hey, she give me love and I feel all right now.

                   F

Yeah! You gotta toss and turn and feel all right,

         B♭   C

And I feel ___ all right, I say yeah, ___(Yeah,) yeah, (yeah,)

Yeah, (Yeah.) yeah, (Yeah.) yeah.

Chorus 1
                              F

'Cause you make me feel (Like a pony.) so good,

(Like a pony.) so good, (Like a pony.) so good,

                          B♭

(Mony, mony.) so fine, ___ (Mony, mony.) so fine,

(Mony, mony.) it's so fine. (Mony, mony.) Well, I feel all right.

                          C

(Mony, mony.) I say yeah, ___ (Yeah.) yeah, (Yeah.) yeah, (Yeah.)

Yeah, (Yeah.) yeah, (Yeah.) yeah. (Yeah.)

Interlude 1

N.C.				
F		B♭	F	B♭

Bridge

    B♭   **F**   **B♭**

‖: (Oo, I love you, mony, mo-mo-mo - ny

              F   **B♭**

Oo, I love you, mony, mo-mo-mo - ny.) :‖ ***Play 4 times***

          C

Say yeah, ___ (Yeah.) yeah, (Yeah.) yeah, (Yeah.) yeah, (Yeah.)

Yeah, (Yeah.) yeah. (Yeah.)

Chorus 2

F

Come on. Come on. Come on. Come on.

B♭

    Come on, come on. Come on, come on.

Come on, come on, feel all right.

        C

I say yeah, ___ (Yeah.) yeah, (Yeah.) yeah, (Yeah.) yeah, (Yeah.)

Yeah, (Yeah.) yeah. (Yeah.)

Interlude 2

F				

Verse 2

     F   **B♭ F**

Wake ___ it, shake it, mony, mony.

                         B♭ F

Shotgun dead and a come on, mony.

                                 B♭ F

Don't stop cookin' 'cause I feel all right now.

        F

Hey! But don't stop now, come on, mony,

     B♭

Come ___ on, yeah.

        C

I say yeah, ___ (Yeah.) yeah, (Yeah.) yeah, (Yeah.) yeah, (Yeah.)

Yeah. (Yeah.)

Chorus 3

> **F**
> 'Cause you make me feel (Like a pony.) so good,
>
> (Like a pony.) so good, (Like a pony.) Well, I feel all right.
>
> **B♭**
> (Mony, mony.)   You so fine, (Mony, mony.) you so fine,
>
> (Mony, mony.) you so fine. (Mony, mony.) I will be all right.
>
> **C**
> (Mony, mony.) I say yeah, ___ (Yeah.) yeah, (Yeah.) yeah, (Yeah.)
>
> **F**
> Yeah, (yeah.) yeah, I wanna   ride your pony, ride your pony,
>
> **B♭**
> Ride your pony. Come on, come on. (Come on!)
>
> Come on, mony. Feel all right.
>
> **C**
> I say yeah, ___ (Yeah.) yeah, (Yeah.) yeah, (Yeah.)
>
> Yeah, (Yeah.) yeah.

Chorus 4

> **F**
> 'Cause you make me feel (Like a pony.) so good,
>
> (Like a pony.) so good, (Like a pony.) so good.
>
> **B♭**
> (Like a pony.)   Come on! (Mony, mony.) Yeah, all right.
>
> (Mony, mony. Mony, mony.) Well, I feel so good.
>
> **C**
> (Mony, mony.) I say yeah, ___ (Yeah.) yeah, (Yeah.) yeah, (Yeah.)
>
> Yeah. (Yeah.)   *Fade out*

Old Time Rock & Roll

Words and Music by George Jackson
and Thomas E. Jones III

Just take those old rec-ords off the shelf, __

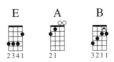

2 3 4 1   2 1   3 2 1 1

Intro | N.C.(E) | N.C. | N.C.(E) |

Verse 1

        N.C.   E
    Just take those old records off the shelf,

                             A
I'll sit and listen to 'em by myself.

                        B
Today's music ain't got the same soul.

                     E
I like that old time rock and roll.

Don't try to take me to a disco,

                     A
You'll never even get me out on the floor.

                     B
In ten minutes I'll be late for the door.

                 E
I like the old time rock and roll.

Chorus 1

B   E
Still like that old time rock and roll,

                   A
That kind of music just soothes the soul.

              B
I reminisce about the days of old

            E   B
With that old time rock and roll.

Guitar Solo

E		A		
B		E		

Verse 2

B   E
Won't go to hear 'em play a Tango.

                 A
I'd rather hear some blues or funky old soul.

              B
There's only one sure way to get me to go;

           E
Start playing old time rock and roll.

Call me a relic, call me what you will.

              A
Say I'm old fashioned, say I'm over the hill.

           B
Today's music ain't got the same soul.

           E
I like that old time rock and roll.

Chorus 2   *Repeat Chorus 1*

Sax Solo   *Repeat Guitar Solo*

Chorus 3

B   **E**
Still like that old time rock and roll,

           A
That kind of music just soothes the soul.

          B
I reminisce about the days of old

         E
With that old time rock and roll.

Chorus 4

B   **N.C.**
Still like that old time rock and roll,

That kind of music just soothes the soul.

I reminisce about the days of old

With that old time rock and roll.

Chorus 5

B   **E**
Still like that old time rock and roll,

          A
That kind of music just soothes the soul.

        B
I reminisce about the days of old

     E
With that old time rock and roll.

B
Still like that old time rock and roll.

B   **E**   **A** **B E B**

Outro-Guitar Solo   Still like that old time rock and roll.

‖: E | | A | |

| B | | E | B   :‖ *Repeat and fade*

Mustang Sally

Words and Music by
Bonny Rice

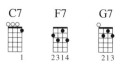

Intro
‖: **C7** | :‖

Verse 1

      C7
Mustang Sal - ly, huh, ha,

Guess you better slow your mustang down.

Oh, Lord. What I said, now.

    F7
Mustang Sally, now baby, oh, Lord,

                       C7
Guess you better slow your mustang down.

           G7
Ha! Oh, yeah. You been runnin' all over town now.

F7 N.C.   **C7**
    Oh! I guess I'll have to put your flat feet on the ground.

Ha! What I said, now.

Chorus 1

C7
Listen! All you wanna do is ride around, Sally. (Ride, Sally, ride.)

All you wanna do is ride around, Sally. (Ride, Sally, ride.)
F7
All you wanna do is ride around, Sally. (Ride, Sally, ride.)
C7
All you wanna do is ride around, Sally. (Ride, Sally, ride.)
G7
One of these early mornin's,

F7 N.C.   C7
  Wow! Gonna be wipin' your weepin' eyes.

Ha! What I said, now. Looky here.

Verse 2

C7
I bought you a brand-new Mustang, a nineteen-sixty-five.

Ha! Now you come around signifying a woman,

You don't wanna let me ride.
     F7
Mustang ____ Sally, now baby, oh, Lord,
           C7
Guess you better slow that mustang ____ down.
         G7
Ha! Oh, Lord. Listen! You been runnin' all over town.
F7 N.C.   C7
  Oh! I got to put your flat feet on the ground.

Ha! What I said, now. Let me say it one more time y'all.

Outro-Chorus   *Repeat Chorus 1 and fade*

No Particular Place to Go

Words and Music by
Chuck Berry

Rid - in' a - long in my au - to - mo - bile,...

D7   G   C7

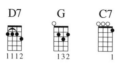

1112   132   1

Intro | D7 |

Verse 1

N.C.   G
Riding along in my automo-bile,

N.C.   G
   My baby beside me at the wheel.

N.C.   C7
   I stole a kiss at the turn of a mile,

N.C.   G
   My curiosity running wild.

N.C.   D7
   Cruising and playing the radi-o,

N.C.   G
   With no particular place to go.

Verse 2

N.C.   G
   Riding along in my automo-bile,

N.C.   G
   I was anxious to tell her the way I feel.

N.C.   C7
   So I told her softly and sin-cere,

N.C.   G
   And she leaned and whispered in my ear.

N.C.   D7
   Cuddlin' more and driving slow,

N.C.   G
   With no particular place to go.

Solo 1		G										
		C				G					
		D		C		G					

Verse 3

N.C.   G
No particular place to go,

N.C.   G
So we parked way out on the Koko-mo.

N.C.   C7
The night was young and the moon was gold,

N.C.   G
So we both decided to take a stroll.

N.C.   D7
Can you imagine the way I felt?

N.C.   G
I couldn't unfasten her seat belt.

Verse 4

N.C.   G
Riding along in my calaboose,

N.C.   G
Still trying to get her belt a loose.

N.C.   C7
All the way home I held a grudge,

N.C.   G
For the safety belt that wouldn't budge.

N.C.   D7
Cruising and playing the radi-o,

N.C.   G
With no particular place to go.

Solo 2   *Repeat Solo 1 (2 times)*

Not Fade Away

Words and Music by
Charles Hardin and Norman Petty

Melody:

I wan-na tell ya how it's __ gon - na be.

E   A   D

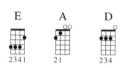

2341   21   234

Intro

|E A E | A E | A E | A E |

Verse 1

E   A   D   A
I wanna tell ya how it's gonna be.

    E   A E   A E
Uh, you're gonna give your love to me.

                        A   D   A
I'm gonna love you night and day.

Chorus 1

    E   A E   A E
Oh, love is love, not fade away.

                          A E
Uh, well, love is love, not fade away.

Verse 2

    E   A   D   A
Uh, my love's bigger than a Cadillac.

    E   A E   A E
I ___try to show it and you drive me back.

                        A   D   A
Uh, your love for me has got to be real,

E   A E   A E
For you to know just how I feel.

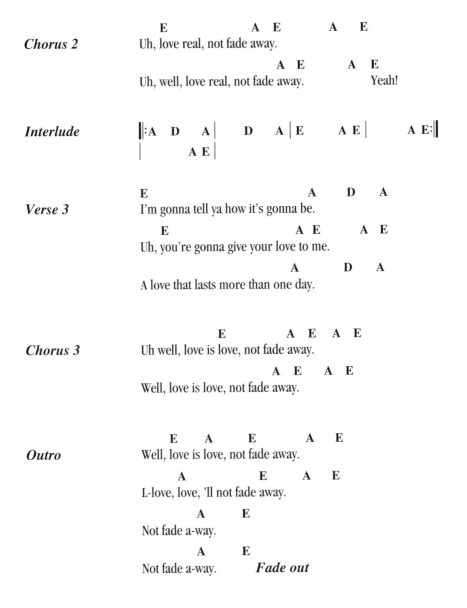

Chorus 2

     E   A E   A   E
Uh, love real, not fade away.

                          A E   A   E
Uh, well, love real, not fade away.   Yeah!

Interlude

‖: A   D   A | D   A | E   A E | A E :‖
| A E |

Verse 3

E   A   D   A
I'm gonna tell ya how it's gonna be.

     E   A E   A   E
Uh, you're gonna give your love to me.

                        A   D   A
A love that lasts more than one day.

Chorus 3

         E   A E A E
Uh well, love is love, not fade away.

                  A E   A E
Well, love is love, not fade away.

Outro

     E   A   E   A   E
Well, love is love, not fade away.

     A   E   A   E
L-love, love, 'll not fade away.

     A   E
Not fade a-way.

     A   E
Not fade a-way.   ***Fade out***

Ring of Fire

Words and Music by
Merle Kilgore and June Carter

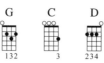

Intro

| G | C | G | | |
| | D | G | |

Verse 1

```
G        C      G     C G
Love is a burning thing
                D G      D G
And it makes its fir - y ring.
              C       G      C G
Bound by wild__ desires,
            D       G
I fell into a ring of fire.
```

Chorus 1

```
D          C              G
I fell into a burning ring of fire.
         D
I went down, down, down
         C        G
And the flames went higher.

And it burns, burns, burns,
       D    G
The ring of fire,
       D    G
The ring of fire.
```

Interlude		G	C	G				
			D	G			

Verse 2

       G   C   G   C G
The taste of love is sweet

                D   G   D G
When hearts like ours meet.

            C   G   C G
I fell for you like a child,

          D   G
Oh, but the fire went wild.

Chorus 2   *Repeat Chorus 1*

Chorus 3   *Repeat Chorus 1*

Outro

        G
And it burns, burns, burns,

        D   G
The ring__of fire,

        D   G
‖: The ring of fire. :‖   *Repeat and fade*

Rock Around the Clock

Words and Music by
Max C. Freedman and Jimmy DeKnight

One, two, three o' clock, four o' clock rock.

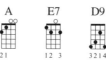

Intro

                                                 A
One, two, three o'clock, four o'clock rock.

        N.C.   **A**
Five, six, seven o'clock, eight o'clock rock.

        N.C.
Nine, ten, eleven o'clock, twelve o'clock rock.

        E7
We're gonna rock around the clock tonight.

Verse 1

        A
Put your glad rags on and join me, hon.

We'll have some fun when the clock strikes one.

        D9
We're gonna rock around the clock tonight.

        A
We're gonna rock, rock, rock 'til broad daylight.

        E7   **A**
We're gonna rock, gonna rock around the clock tonight.

Verse 2

        A
When the clock strikes two, three and four,

If the band slows down we'll yell for more.

        D9
We're gonna rock around the clock tonight.

        A
We're gonna rock, rock, rock 'til broad daylight.

        E7   **A**
We're gonna rock, gonna rock around the clock tonight.

Solo   *Repeat Verse 1 (Instrumental)*

Verse 3
       A
When the chimes ring five and six and seven

We'll be right in seventh heav'n.
       D9
We're gonna rock around the clock tonight.
       A
We're gonna rock, rock, rock 'til broad daylight.
       E7   **A**
We're gonna rock, gonna rock around the clock tonight.

Verse 4
       A
When it's eight, nine, ten, eleven too,

I'll be goin' strong and so will you.
       D9
We're gonna rock around the clock tonight.
       A
We're gonna rock, rock, rock 'til broad daylight.
       E7   **A**
We're gonna rock, gonna rock around the clock tonight.

Verse 5
       A
When the clock strike twelve, we'll cool off then,

Start a rockin' 'round the clock again.
       D9
We're gonna rock around the clock tonight.
       A
We're gonna rock, rock, rock 'til broad daylight.
       E7   **A**
We're gonna rock, gonna rock around the clock tonight.

Rock This Town

Words and Music by
Brian Setzer

Melody:

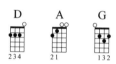

Well, my ba-by and me __ went out late

D   A   G

2 3 4   2 1   1 3 2

Intro   ‖: D | | | :‖ *Play 3 times*

Verse 1
        D
Well, my baby and me went out late Saturday night.

                                          A
I had my hair piled tight and my baby just looked so right.

        D
Well, pick you up at ten, gotta have you home at two.

        G
Your mama don't know what I got in store for you.

          D   **A**
But that's ____ all right 'cause we're lookin' as cool as can be.

Interlude 1   ‖: N.C.(D) | | | :‖

Verse 2
        D
Well, we found a little place that really didn't look half bad.

                                          A
I had a whiskey on the rocks and change of a dollar for the jukebox.

        D
Well, I put a quarter right into that can,

        G
But all it played was disco, man.

          D   **A**   **D**
Come on, ____ pretty baby, let's get out of here right away.

Chorus 1

            D
We're gonna rock this town, rock it inside out.

                                             A
We're gonna rock this town, make 'em scream and shout.

            D
Let's rock, rock, rock, man rock.

            G
We're gonna rock till we pop, we're gonna roll till we drop.

            D   **A**   **D**
We're gonna rock this town, rock ___ it inside out.

Guitar Solo 1   *Repeat Verse 1 (Instrumental)*

Interlude 2   *Repeat Interlude 1*

Verse 3

            D
Well, we're havin' a ball just a boppin' on the big dance floor.

                                             A
Well, there's a real square cat; he looks of nineteen seventy-four.

            D   **N.C.**   **D**   **N.C.**
Well, you look at me once, you look at me twice.

G   **N.C.**   **G**
Look at me again and there's gonna be a fight.

            D   **A**   **D**
We're gonna rock this town, we're gonna rip this place apart.

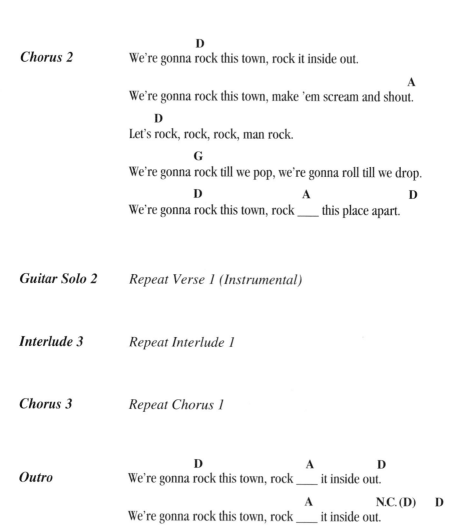

Chorus 2

          D
We're gonna rock this town, rock it inside out.

                                            A
We're gonna rock this town, make 'em scream and shout.

          D
Let's rock, rock, rock, man rock.

          G
We're gonna rock till we pop, we're gonna roll till we drop.

          D   A   D
We're gonna rock this town, rock ___ this place apart.

Guitar Solo 2   *Repeat Verse 1 (Instrumental)*

Interlude 3   *Repeat Interlude 1*

Chorus 3   *Repeat Chorus 1*

Outro

          D   A   D
We're gonna rock this town, rock ___ it inside out.

                                    A   N.C.(D)   D
We're gonna rock this town, rock ___ it inside out.

See You Later, Alligator

Words and Music by
Robert Guidry

Well, I saw my ba-by walk-in'

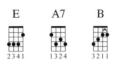

Verse 1

N.C.   E
Well, I saw my baby walkin'

With another man today.

         A7
Well, I saw my baby walkin'

         E
With another man to-day.

         B
When I ask her, "What's the matter?"

         E
This is what I heard her say,

Chorus 1

N.C.   E
  See you later, alli - gator.

After while, crocodile.

         A7
See you later, alli - gator.

         E
After while, croco - dile.

         B
Can't you see you're in my way now?

         E
Don't you know you cramp my style?

Verse 2

N.C.   **E**
When I thought of what she told me,

Nearly made me lose my head.
                       A7
When I thought of what she told me,
                    E
Nearly made me lose my head.
                 B
But the next time that I saw her,
                  E
Reminded her of what she said.

Chorus 2   *Repeat Chorus 1*

Guitar Solo

E					
A7		**E**		
B		**E**		

Verse 3

N.C.   **E**
She said, "I'm sorry, pretty daddy,

You know my love is just for you."
                     A7
She said, "I'm sorry, pretty daddy,
                   E
You know my love is just for you.
                B
Won't you say that you for - give me
                E
And say your love for me is true?"

Verse 4

N.C.   E
  I said, "Wait a minute, 'gator,

I know you mean it just for play."

            A7
I said, "Wait a minute, 'gator,

                E
I know you mean it just for play."

                B
Don't you know you really hurt me?

              E
And this is what I have to say…

Chorus 3   *Repeat Chorus 1*

Chorus 4

N.C.   E
  See you later, alli - gator.

After while crocodile.

           A7
See you later, alli - gator.

           B   E
So long, that's all, ___ goodbye!

Stir It Up

Words and Music by
Bob Marley

Melody:

Stir _ it up, ___   lit - tle dar - ling.

A   D   E

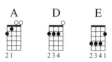

2 1   2 3 4   2 3 4 1

Intro ‖: A | D E :‖ *Play 4 times*

Chorus 1
    A   D   E   A   D   E
Stir it up,   little darling, stir it up. Come on baby.

                  A   D   E   A   D E
Come on and stir it up,   little darling, stir it up.

Verse 1
               A
It's been a long, long time

   D   E   A   D   E
   Since I've got you on my mind. (Ooh)

     A
And now you are here.

     D   E   A
I say it's so clear to see what a we will do, baby.

   D   E
   Just me and you.

Chorus 2   *Repeat Chorus 1*

              A   D   E

Verse 2   I'll push the wood, and I'll blaze your fire.

              A   D   E

           Then I'll satisfy your   all de - sire.

              A   D   E

           Said I stir it, yeah,   ev'ry minute.

              A   D   E

           All you've got to do, baby,   is keep it in it and

Chorus 3   *Repeat Chorus 1*

                  A   D   E

Verse 3   And then   quench me   when I'm thirsty.

              A   D   E

           Come on, cool me down, ba - by, when I'm hot.

              A   D   E

           Your recipe, darling,   is so tasty.

              A   D   E

           And you sure   can stir your pot.

Chorus 4   *Repeat Chorus 1 (w/ voc. ad lib.) and Fade*

Surfin' U.S.A.

Words and Music by
Chuck Berry

Melody:

If ev - 'ry - bod - y had an o - cean... _

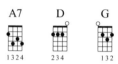

A7   D   G

1324   234   132

Verse 1

N.C.   A7   N.C.   D
If everybody had an ocean   across the U.S.A.

N.C.   A7   N.C.   D
Then ev'rybody'd be surfin',   like California.

N.C.   G
You'd see them wearin' their bag - gies,

N.C.   D
Huarachi sandals too.

N.C.   A7
A bushy, bushy blond hairdo,

G N.C.   D
Surfin' U.S.A.

                      A7   D
You'll catch 'em surfin' at Del Mar, Ventura County Line,

        A7   D
Santa Cruz and Tressels, Australia's Narabine,

       G   D
All over Man-hattan and down Doheny way.

          A7   G N.C.   D
Ev'rybody's gone surfin',   surfin' U.S.A.

Verse 2

    N.C.   A7
    We'll all be plannin' out a route

    N.C.   D
    We're gonna take real soon,

    N.C.   A7
    We're waxing down our surf boards,

    N.C.   D
    We can't wait for June.

    N.C.   G
    We'll all be gone for the sum - mer,

    N.C.   D
    We're on safari to stay.

    N.C.   A7
    Tell the teacher we're surfin',

G N.C.   D
    Surfin' U.S.A.

                  A7   D
At Haggarty's and Swami's, Pacific Palisades,

                  A7   D
San Onofre and Sunset Redondo Beach, L.A.

                G   D
All over La Jol - la, and at Waiamea Bay.

                A7
Ev'rybody's gone surfin',

G N.C.   D
    Surfin' U.S.A.

              A7
Outro ||: Ev'rybody's gone surfin',

G N.C.   D
    Surfin' U.S.A.   :|| *Repeat and fade*

Sweet Home Chicago

Words and Music by
Robert Johnson

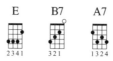

Intro |E | | |B7 |

Chorus 1

      E A7   E
Come on, baby, don't cha wanna go?

        A7   E
Come on, ____ baby, don't cha wanna go

        B7   A7   E B7
Back to that same old place,   sweet home Chi - cago?

Chorus 2

      E A7   E
Come on, baby, don't cha wanna go?

        A7   E
Highdee hey, baby, don't cha wanna go

        B7   A7   E B7
Back to that same old place,   sweet home Chi - cago?

Verse 1

  E N.C.   **E N.C.**
Well, one and one is two, six and two is eight.

E **N.C.**   **E**
 Come on, baby, don't cha make me late!

   A7   **E**
Highdee hey, baby, don't cha wanna go

    B7   **A7**   **E** **B7**
Back to that same old place, sweet home Chi - cago?

Chorus 3   *Repeat Chorus 1*

Guitar Solo

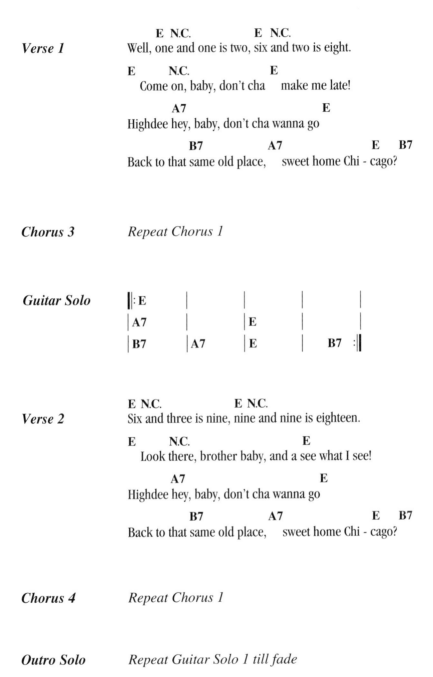

```
‖: E        |           |           |           |
 | A7       |           | E         |           |
 | B7       | A7        | E         |           | B7   :‖
```


Verse 2

  E N.C.   **E N.C.**
Six and three is nine, nine and nine is eighteen.

E **N.C.**   **E**
 Look there, brother baby, and a see what I see!

   A7   **E**
Highdee hey, baby, don't cha wanna go

    B7   **A7**   **E** **B7**
Back to that same old place, sweet home Chi - cago?

Chorus 4   *Repeat Chorus 1*

Outro Solo   *Repeat Guitar Solo 1 till fade*

Thirty Days in the Hole

Words and Music by Steve Marriott

Melody:

Chi - ca - go___ Green,___

E   A   D

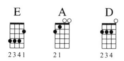

2 3 4 1   2 1   2 3 4

Intro | E | | A   E | | | | |

Verse 1
       A   E
Chi-cago Green,

          A   E
Talkin' 'bout Black Leba-nese,

  A   E   A   E
A dirty room___ and a silver coke spoon,

  A   E
     Give me my re-lease.

  A   E
Black Nepa-lese,

         A   E
It's got you weak in your knees.

  A   E   A   E
Seize some dust that you got bust on;

     D   A
You know it's hard to be-lieve.

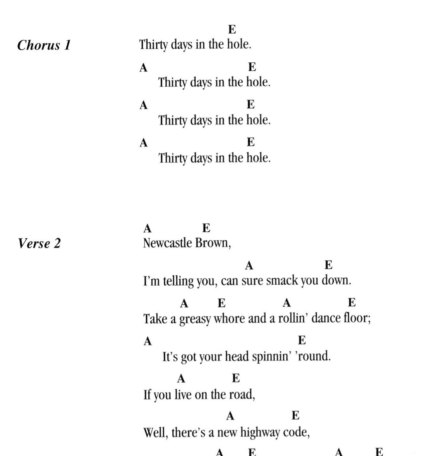

Chorus 1

                  E
Thirty days in the hole.

A   E
   Thirty days in the hole.

A   E
   Thirty days in the hole.

A   E
   Thirty days in the hole.

Verse 2

A   E
Newcastle Brown,

             A   E
I'm telling you, can sure smack you down.

       A   E   A   E
Take a greasy whore and a rollin' dance floor;

A   E
   It's got your head spinnin' 'round.

      A   E
If you live on the road,

         A   E
Well, there's a new highway code,

        A E   A   E
You take the urban noise, with some Durban Poi-son,

D   A
   It's gonna lessen your load.

Chorus 2   **Repeat Chorus 1**

Verse 3

   A   E
Black Nepa-lese,

     A   E
It's got you weak in your knees.

    A   E
Gonna seize some dust

    A   E
That you got bust on,

A   E
 You know it's so hard to please.

A E
Newcastle Brown,

   A   E
Can sure smack you down.

    A E
You take a greasy whore,

    A   E
And a rollin' dance floor,

D   A
 You know you're jailhouse bound.

Chorus 3   ***Repeat Chorus 1 till fade***

Time for Me to Fly

Words and Music by Kevin Cronin

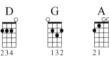

Intro ‖: D G | A G :‖

Verse 1
    D
I've been around for you,

     A
I've been up and down for you,

     G   **D G D G D**
But I__ just can't get any relief.

I've swallowed my pride for you,

A
     Lived and lied for you,

     G   **D G D G D**
But a you still make me feel like a thief.

       A
You got me stealin' your love away

     G   **D**
'Cause a you never give it.

A
Peelin' the years away

     G   **D**
And a we can't re-live it.

   G   **D**
Oh, I make you laugh,

   G   **D**
And a you make me cry.

A
    I believe it's time for me to fly.

‖: D   G | A   G   :‖

Verse 2

D
You said we'd work it out,

   A
You said that you had no doubt,

   G   **D   G   D   G**
That deep down we were really in love.

D
Oh, but I'm tired of holdin' on

   A
To feelin' I know is gone.

G   **D   G   D   G**
   I do believe that I've had enough.

   D   **A**
I've had e-nough of the falseness

     G   **D**
Of a worn - out re-lation.

   A
E-nough of the jealousy

     G   **D**
And the intolera - tion.

   G   **D**
Oh, I make you laugh,

     G   **D**
And a you make me cry.

A   **D   G   D   N.C.**
   I believe it's time for me to fly.

Chorus 1

                   A   **G**   **D**
(Time for me to fly.)

                       Oh, I've got to set__ myself free.

                   A   **G**   **D**
(Time for me to fly.)

                       Ah, that's just how it's a got to   be.

G   A
   I know it hurts to say good-bye,

                          G   A
But it's time for me to fly.

Interlude |D | |G | | |
                |A | |D | |

                         A   G   D

Chorus 2   (Time for me to fly.)
                         Oh, I've got to set__ myself free.
                       A   G   D
   (Time for me to fly.)
                      Ah, that's just how it's a got to   be.

G   A
   I know it hurts to say good-bye,

                        G   A
But it's time for me to fly.

                    G   A
It's time for me to fly,__ ee-i, ee-i.

                   D
It's time for me to fly.

            G   A
(It's time for me to fly.)

            G   D
It's time for me to fly.

                A
(It's time for me to fly.)

            G   D
It's time for me to fly.

            G   A   G   D
(It's time for me to fly.)
                   Babe,__ it's time for me to fly.

Tulsa Time

Words and Music by
Danny Flowers

Melody:

I ___ left Ok-la-ho-ma driv - in' in a Pon-ti - ac,

Intro | E | | |

Verse 1

         E
I ____ left Oklahoma drivin' in a Pontiac,

               B
Just about to lose my mind.

I was goin' to Arizona, maybe on to California

               E
Where the people all live so fine.

My baby said I's crazy, my Momma called me lazy,

              B
I was goin' to show 'em all this time,

'Cause you know I ain't no foolin', I don't need no more schoolin',

            E
I was born to just walk the line.

Chorus 1

E   **B**
Livin' on Tulsa time. Livin' on Tulsa time.

Well, you know I been thru it when I set my watch back to it,

          E
Livin' on Tulsa time.

Dobro Solo		E								**B**			
							E	

Verse 2

        E
Well, there I was in Hollywood wishin' I was doin' good,

                B
Talkin' on the telephone line.

But they don't need me in the movies and nobody sings my songs,

             E
Guess I'm just a-wastin' time.

Well, then I got to thinkin', man, I'm really sinkin'

              B
And I really had a flash this time.

I had no business leavin' and nobody would be grievin'

           E
If I went on back to Tulsa time.

Chorus 2

    E   B
‖: Livin'on Tulsa time. Livin' on Tulsa time.

Gonna set my watch back to it, 'cause you know I've been thru it,

         E
Livin' on Tulsa time. :‖

Outro   ***Repeat Dobro Solo and fade***

Tutti Frutti

Words and Music by
Little Richard Penniman and Dorothy La Bostrie

Melody:

A bop bop a loom op a lop bop boom!

F   B♭7   C7

2 1   1 2 1 1   1

Intro

N.C.
A bop bop a loom op

A lop bop boom!

Chorus 1

F
Tutti frutti, au rutti,

Tutti frutti, au rutti.

B♭7
Tutti frutti, au rutti,

F
Tutti frutti, au rutti.

C7   B♭7
Tutti frutti, au rutti.

F N.C.
A bop bop a loom op

A lop bop boom!

Verse 1	**F** I got a gal, her name's Sue,	

She knows just what to do.

    Bb7
I got a gal, her name's Sue,

    F
She knows just what to do.

        N.C.   **F N.C.**
She's rocked to the east, she's rocked to the west,

    F N.C.
But she's the gal I love the best.

Chorus 2   *Repeat Chorus 1*

Verse 2   **F**
I got a gal, her name's Daisy,

She almost drives me crazy.

    Bb7
I got a gal, her name's Daisy,

    F
She almost drives me crazy.

        N.C.   **F N.C.**
She knows how to love me, yes, indeed.

F N.C.
Boy, you don't know what you do to me.

Chorus 3   *Repeat Chorus 1*

Solo   *Repeat Chorus 1 (Instrumental)*

Chorus 4   *Repeat Chorus 1*

Verse 3   *Repeat Verse 2*

Chorus 5   *Repeat Chorus 1*

The Twist

Words and Music by
Hank Ballard

Come on, ba - by,...

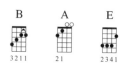

Intro | B | A | E | |

Verse 1
                           E
Come on, ba - by, let's do the twist.

                 A   E
Come on, ba - by, let's do the twist.

                     B   A   E
Take me by my little hand   and go like this.

Chorus 1
              E
Ee ah. Twist, babe, baby, twist.

              A
Woo. Yeah.

           E
Just like this.

                    B   A N.C.   E
Come on, little miss,___   and do the twist.

Verse 2

> E
> My daddy is sleep - in' and mama ain't around.
>
>   A   E
> Yeah, daddy's just sleep - in' and mama ain't around.
>
>   B
> We're gonna twist, a twist, a twistin',
>
> A N.C.   E
> Till we tear the house down.

Chorus 2

Repeat Chorus 1

Solo

Repeat Chorus 1 (Instrumental)

Verse 3

>   E
> Yeah, you should see__ my little sis.
>
>   A   E
> You should see__ my, my little sis.
>
>   B
> She really knows how to rock,
>
> A N.C.   E
> She knows how to twist.

Chorus 3

Repeat Chorus 1

Outro

Repeat Chorus 1 (Instrumental)

Up Around the Bend

Words and Music by
John Fogerty

There's a place __ up a - head __ and I'm go - in'

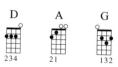

D   A   G
2 3 4   2 1   1 3 2

Intro

‖: D | | A | D :‖

Verse 1

D
There's a place up ahead and I'm goin'
A   D
Just as fast as my feet can fly.

Come away, come away if you're goin',
A   D
Leave the sinkin' ship be - hind.

Chorus 1

G   D   A
Come on the risin' wind,
     G   D   A
We're goin' up a - round the bend. ____ Oo!

Verse 2

D
Bring a song and a smile for the banjo.
A   D
Better get while the gettin's good.

Hitch a ride to the end of the highway
A   D
Where the neons turn to wood.

Chorus 2

Repeat Chorus 1

Verse 3

D
    You can ponder perpetual motion,

A   D
    Fix your mind on a crystal day.

Always time for a good conversation,

A   D
    There's an ear for what you say.

Chorus 3

G   D   A
Come on the risin' wind,

      G   D   A
We're goin' up a - round the bend. ___ Yeah!

Interlude

‖: D | | A | D   :‖

Guitar Solo

|G   D |A |G   D |A | |
                                           Oo! ___

Verse 4

D
    Catch a ride to the end of the highway

A   D
    And we'll meet by the big red tree.

There's a place up ahead and I'm goin';

A   D
Come along, come along with me.

Chorus 4

Repeat Chorus 3

Outro

‖: D
    Doot, doot, do, do.

A   D
    Doot, doot do, do, do. :‖ ***Repeat and fade***

Werewolves of London

Words and Music by Warren Zevon,
Robert Wachtel and LeRoy Marinel

I saw a were-wolf with a Chi-nese men-u in his hand

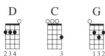

D   C   G

Intro ‖: D C | G :‖ *Play 4 times*

Verse 1

```
D                  C              G
I saw a were - wolf with a Chinese menu in his hand
D                          C      G
Walkin' through the streets ___ of Soho ___ in the rain.
D        C                      G
He was lookin' for the place called Li Ho Fook's.
D        C              G
Gonna get a big dish of beef chow mein.
```

Chorus 1

```
D    C   G              D    C G
Ow ooh, werewolves of London,  ow ooh.
D    C   G              D    C G
Ow ooh, werewolves of London,  ow ooh.
```

Verse 2

```
D               C              G
You hear him howlin' around your kitchen door,
D    C              G
You better not let him in.
D        C                  G
Little old lady got mutilated late last night.
D            C          G
Werewolves of London again.
```

Chorus 2   *Repeat Chorus 1*

Guitar Solo   *Repeat Verse 1 (Instrumental)*

Verse 3
```
        D                    C      G
He's the hairy handed gent    who ran amuck at Kent.
D               C                 G
Lately he's been o - verheard in May - fair.
D                 C              G
  You better stay a - way from him,    he'll rip your lungs out, Jim.
D        C                    G
Huh! I'd like to meet his tailor.
```

Chorus 3   *Repeat Chorus 1*

Verse 4
```
D  C                    G
I saw Lon Chaney walk - in' with the Queen
D           C               G
Doin' the werewolves of Lon - don.
D        C                  G
I saw ___ Lon Chaney junior ___ walkin' with the Queen, uh,
D            C              G
Doin' the were - wolves of Lon - don.
D         C                  G
I saw a werewolf drinking a Pina Colada at Trader Vic's
D           C              G
And his hair was perfect.
```

Outro
```
D     C G
Ow ooh,
D C                      G
  Werewolves of Lon - don. Huh, draw blood.
D     C G
Ow ooh,
D C                 G   D C G
  Werewolves of Lon - don.    Fade out
```

Wooly Bully

Words and Music by
Domingo Samudio

Melody:

Mat-ty told Hat-ty   a-bout a

G7   C7   D7

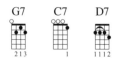

Intro

N.C.
Spoken: *Uno, dos, one, two, tres, quatro.*

|G7 | | | |

|G7 | | | |
Hey, Wooly, Bully. Watch it, now, watch it.   Here he come,
|C7 | |
Here he come.
|G7 | |D7 |C7 |G7 |
Watch it, now, he get you.

Verse 1

G7
Matty told Hatty about a thing she saw.

Had two big horns and a wooly jaw.

Chorus 1

C7   G7
Wooly Bully, Wooly Bully.
D7   C7   G7   D7
Wooly Bully, Wooly Bully, Wooly Bully.

Verse 2	**G7** Hatty told Matty, "Let's don't take no chance, Let's not be L-seven, come and learn to dance."
Chorus 2	*Repeat Chorus 1*
Interlude	$\mid$ **G7**　　$\mid$　　　$\mid$　　　$\mid$
Sax Solo	*Repeat Verse 1 and Chorus 1*
Verse 3	**G7** Matty told Hatty, "It's the thing to do Get you someone, really pull the wool with you."
Chorus 3	*Repeat Chorus 1*
Outro	$\mid$ **G7**　　$\mid$　　　$\mid$　　$\mid$ N.C. $\parallel$

You Are My Sunshine

Words and Music by
Jimmie Davis

Melody:

The oth - er night dear... ____

E   A   B7

Verse 1

             E
The other night dear as I lay sleeping,

          A   E
I dreamed I held you in my arms.

        A   E
When I a-woke dear I was mis-taken,

         B7   E
And I hung my head and cried:

Chorus 1

            E
You are my sunshine, my only sunshine,

        A   E
You make me happy when skies are gray.

        A   E
You'll never know dear how much I love you.

        B7   E
Please don't take my sunshine a-way.

Verse 2

        E
I'll always love you and make you happy,

      A   **E**
If you will only say the same.

      A   **E**
But if you leave me to love an-other

        B7   **E**
You'll regret it all some day.

Chorus 2   ***Repeat Chorus 1***

Verse 3

        E
You told me once dear you really loved me,

      A   **E**
And no one else could come be-tween.

       A   **E**
But now you've left me and love an-other;

       B7   **E**
You have shattered all my dreams.

Chorus 3   ***Repeat Chorus 1***

Your Mama Don't Dance

Words and Music by
Jim Messina and Kenny Loggins

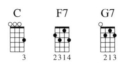

Intro ‖: C | | | :‖

Chorus 1

          C   F7   C
Your mama don't dance and your daddy don't rock 'n roll.

  F7   C
Your mama don't dance and your daddy don't rock 'n roll.

  G7   F7
When ev'nin' rolls around and it's time to go to town,

              C
Where do you go to rock 'n roll?

Verse 1

          C   F7   C
The old folks say that you gotta end your date by ten.

      F7   C
If you're out on a date and you bring it home late, it's a sin.

   G7   F7   C
There just ain't no excuse and you know you're gonna lose and never win.

                N.C.
I'll say it again. And it's all because…

Chorus 2   *Repeat Chorus 1*

Sax Solo   *Repeat Chorus 1 (Instrumental)*

Guitar Solo   *Repeat Chorus 1 (Instrumental)*

                      F7
Bridge   You pull into a drive-in and find a place to park.

You hop into the back seat where you know it's nice and dark.

You're just about to move and you're thinkin' it's a breeze,

There's a light in your eye and then a guy says,

          N.C.   G7   F7
"Out of the car, long hair!" Ooh-whee! ____ "You're coming with me!"

               C N.C.
The local police! ____   And it's all because....

Chorus 3   *Repeat Chorus 1*

                    C
Outro   Where do you go to rock 'n roll?

                         N.C. C
Where do you go to rock 'n roll?

Twist and Shout

Words and Music by
Bert Russell and Phil Medley

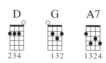

Intro |D   G   A7| |D   G   A7| |

Chorus 1

                   D
Well, shake it up ba - by, now,

G   **A7**
(Shake it up, baby.)

         D
Twist and shout.

G   **A7**
(Twist and shout.)

                     D
Come on, come on, come on, come on, baby now.

G   **A7**
(Come on, baby.)

             D
Come on and work it on out.

G   **A7**
(Work it on out.)

Verse 1

                                                  D
Well, work it on out.

G   **A7**
(Work it on out.)

                             D
You know you look so good.

G   **A7**
(Look so good.)

                        D
You know you got me goin' now.

G   **A7**
(Got me goin'.)

                           D
Just like I knew you would.

        G   **A7**
(Like I knew you would. Oo.)

Chorus 2

Repeat Chorus 1

Verse 2

                               D
You know you twist, little girl.

G   **A7**
(Twist little girl.)

                        D
You know you twist so fine.

G   **A7**
(Twist so fine.)

                           D
Come on and twist a little closer now,

G   **A7**
(Twist a little closer.)

                           D
And let me know that you're mine.

        G   **A7**
(Let me know you're mine, ooh.)

| Interlude | ‖: D   G   A7 \| G   A7 :‖ *Play 4 times* |

Ah, ah, ah, ah. Wow!

Chorus 3   ***Repeat Chorus 1***

Verse 3   ***Repeat Verse 2***

Outro

                                D
Well, shake it, shake it, shake it, baby, now.
G   **A7**
(Shake it up, baby.)

                                D
Well, shake it, shake it, shake, it, baby, now.
G   **A7**
(Shake it up, baby. Oo.)

                        D
Ah, ah, ah, ah.

UKULELE CHORD SONGBOOKS

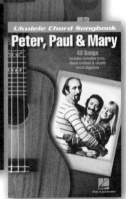

This series features convenient 6" x 9" books with complete lyrics and chord symbols for dozens of great songs. Each song also includes chord grids at the top of every page and the first notes of the melody for easy reference.

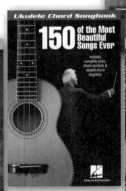

ACOUSTIC ROCK
00702482 . . . . $14.99

THE BEATLES
00703065 . . . . $19.99

BEST SONGS EVER
00117050 . . . . $16.99

CHILDREN'S SONGS
00702473 . . . . $14.99

CHRISTMAS CAROLS
00702474 . . . . $14.99

CHRISTMAS SONGS
00101776 . . . . $14.99

ISLAND SONGS
00702471 . . . . $16.99

150 OF THE MOST BEAUTIFUL SONGS EVER
00117051 . . . . $24.99

PETER, PAUL & MARY
00121822 . . . . $12.99

THREE CHORD SONGS
00702483 . . . . $14.99

TOP HITS
00115929 . . . . $14.99

HAL•LEONARD®
CORPORATION
7777 W. BLUEMOUND RD. P.O. BOX 13819 MILWAUKEE, WI 53213

www.halleonard.com

Prices, contents, and availability
subject to change without notice.

0514